The Teaching for Social Justice Series

William Ayers—Series Editor
Therese Quinn—Associate Series Editor

Editorial Board: Hal Adams, Barbara Bowman, Lisa Delpit, Michelle Fine, Maxine Greene, Caroline Heller, Annette Henry, Asa Hilliard (1933–2007), Rashid Khalidi, Kevin Kumashiro, Gloria Ladson-Billings, Charles Payne, Mark Perry, Luis Rodriguez, Jonathan Silin, William Watkins

The Seduction of Common Sense

How the Right Has Framed the Debate on America's Schools

KEVIN K. KUMASHIRO

Foreword by Herbert Kohl

TEACHERS COLLEGE PRESS

Teachers College
Columbia University
New York and London

April 2008
Dear Maggie—
Thanks so much
for everything!
Love,
Kevin

Permissions:

"Detraction, Fear, and Assimilation: Race, Sexuality, and Education Reform Post–9/11," originally published in *Subaltern Speak: Curriculum, Power, and Educational Struggles* (M. W. Apple & K. L. Buras, Eds.), copyright 2005 by Routledge Publishing Inc., is reproduced with permission of Routledge Publishing Inc.

"Education Policy and Family Values: A Critical Analysis of Initiatives from the Right," was published originally in *Multicultural Perspectives*, copyright 2008 by Taylor & Francis, is available online at http://www.informaworld.com, and is reproduced with permission of Taylor & Francis.

Published by Teachers College Press, 1234 Amsterdam Avenue, New York, NY 10027

Library of Congress Cataloging-in-Publication Data

Kumashiro, Kevin K., 1970–
    The seduction of common sense : how the right has framed the debate on America's schools / Kevin K. Kumashiro ; foreword by Jonathan Kozol.
    p. cm. — (Teaching for social justice series)
    Includes bibliographical references and index.
    ISBN 978-0-8077-4868-8 (pbk. : alk. paper)
    ISBN 978-0-8077-4869-5 (hardcover : alk. paper)
    1. Education—Political aspects—United States. 2. Right and left (Political science)—United States. 3. Conservatism—United States. I. Title.
    LC89.K86 2008
    379.73—dc22   2007045679

ISBN 978-0-8077-4868-8 (paper)
ISBN 978-0-8077-4869-5 (hardcover)

Printed on acid-free paper
Manufactured in the United States of America

15 14 13 12 11 10 09 08   8 7 6 5 4 3 2 1

To my dad
Kenneth Kenji Kumashiro
(1935–2003)

Contents

Series Foreword

Two young fish were swimming upstream when they passed an old crab sitting on a rock in the mud. "How's the water?" asked the crab. The youngsters looked at one another blankly. "What's water?" they asked.

That's a variation on a universal joke whose meaning is, ironically, self-evident: The fish are the last to either notice or be able to describe the water, whose dimensions—texture and temperature, chemical code, resonance, and resistance—nonetheless constitute their whole world. Because they live within the water, it's entirely taken for granted; because they can't quite imagine a non-watery world, they have a distorted view of their own. What's water?

Kevin Kumashiro—full of heart and hope and energy—is in one respect like the old crab on the rock in the mud: His straightforward, simple-sounding questions become gently echoing depth charges lobbed into our hitherto comfortable streams of consciousness. The initial explosion wakes us up; the resonating ripples urge us toward new voyages. Suddenly the conventional is not so settled, received thinking not so acceptable—we are awakened to what is right in front of our eyes.

This book invites us to step outside the water as it were, to suspend disbelief, to look at our world anew, to question our common sense—once so insistent, so powerful, so domineering and dogmatic. Our imaginations are freed to consider alternatives, and the "way things are" seems suddenly inadequate, "the way it's supposed to be," unacceptable. Kevin Kumashiro's aim and accomplishment here are to rearrange our perceptual fields, to invite us to see differently so that we might act differently.

So much of educational practice and school reform—as well as the law, evolving legal standards, and public policy—turns on questions of competing analogies, or what Kevin Kumashiro here refers to as frames. Take an issue roiling the political waters today: healthcare. If the controlling analogy is that healthcare is a *product* much like a television set, then our current system makes some sense—it taps into deeply held cultural beliefs about individual responsibility and choice and cost. But if the analogy shifts, if healthcare begins to be discussed more and more widely as a universal human *right*, like the right to an education or to public safety, then other deeply held beliefs—about fairness and shared or community responsibility—move to the front.

Or take another hotly contested issue: same-sex marriage. If same-sex marriage is like a man hooking up with his cat, it is easily dismissed as "unnatural" and "sick." (And, parenthetically, "interracial" marriage was illegal in much of the United States for more than a century because it was "unnatural.") But if, on the other hand, homosexual love is like all other human love, filled with desire and joy and surprise and ecstasy and connection and confusion and contradiction, well, then, two people who want to get married might just as well do it.

The so-called "war on terror" might illustrate the point from a slightly different angle. The "war on terror" metaphor was constructed in the aftermath of the terrible crimes of September 11, 2001, but it wasn't an inevitable choice. A different metaphor—a criminal justice metaphor, say—might have led to a different conclusion; after all, if there's a killing in Chicago, the cops question witnesses, gather evidence, pursue leads, focus energy and activity on finding the perpetrator. Perhaps the "war on terror," like "the war on poverty" or the "war on drugs," appealed simply because the rhetoric seems to stand for "an all-out effort" or "a serious undertaking." But here the metaphor is brought to life through full-scale military invasions in Afghanistan and Iraq. The metaphoric bind is this: "The war on terror" can't be won because it's being fought against a chimera (a tactic, perhaps, a state of mind, a condition like nervousness: "the war on nervousness"); the real wars in real countries are hard to stop because "the war on terror" is ongoing—it's a war that is everywhere and nowhere at once, a war whose conclusion no one can describe with any confidence.

Challenging the controlling analogy is always a risky business—it involves disrupting unanticipated but linked fields, and it raises related questions. If universal healthcare is a human right, what else might be? If gay people deserve equal treatment before the law, what other groups of people will expect the same? If the "war on terror" is a myth, what else in our public life is rendered unreliable? We enter an open space of rethinking and negotiation—a space where we must rely not on rules so much as on our moral intuition, our commitment to the dignity of persons, our belief in equality, and, yes, our reordered and evolving common sense.

Absent this capacity to raise risky questions and challenge the common conventions of our times, we likely would be burning witches and suffering slavery today. But the capacity to wonder and to challenge belongs to all of us—making and remaking meaning is part of the human condition—and it is the special province of teachers, scholars, artists, educators, and school people. We are called to resist dogma, to expand inquiry, to raise queer questions. Our vocation is to try to shake ourselves and others free of the seductions and anesthetizing effects of the modern predicament, and that includes the seduction of common sense. This is easier said than done, of course, but in this book Kevin Kumashiro provides some hopeful guideposts.

Ours is an age of profit-driven mass media linked to rampant mass consumerism, of celebrity towering over accomplishment, of material goods equated to human value. It is a time of empire resurrected and unapologetic, of permanent war, of rights compromised and undermined, of scapegoating and regression, of bread and circuses and widespread distractions. It is also a time of open questioning, of disenchantment and hope, of searching for the new. It is a time when fundamental questions assume greater urgency: Who do we want to be as a people? What are our responsibilities as citizens? What is the proper role of schools in a democracy? This book is a vital resource as we trudge toward freedom.

—William C. Ayers, University of Illinois at Chicago
—Therese Quinn, The School of the Art Insititue of Chicago

Foreword

Kevin Kumashiro's *The Seduction of Common Sense* is a bold and very interesting attempt to develop a theory that can account for the Right wing stealing the educational agenda. He talks about how the framing of the issues influences public opinion, and goes on to propose ways in which the Left can reframe the same issues in a way that is convincing to people who are worried about the future of children and schools.

One of the most important aspects of the book is Kumashiro's analysis of the way the Right has used fear as a weapon to cloud people's minds—fear of "minorities," of failure to come up to standards, of "failing" schools, and of White children losing their competitive advantages in the school system as currently constituted.

The Seduction of Common Sense is fundamentally about facing these fears and developing strategies to reframe educational issues based on hope and possibility. It is important to take Kumashiro's ideas seriously but, in the current cynical educational climate, to realize that progressive change will not come quickly or easily. But this book is important as we figure out how to fight back and reaffirm the value of a child's life and the importance of creative and humane education.

—Herbert Kohl

Acknowledgments

I hope that I can remember everyone who helped to make this book possible (and I deeply apologize to anyone whom I temporarily forget).

Thank you to my current colleagues at the University of Illinois–Chicago, College of Education, especially our most fab dean Vicki Chou, for providing the resources needed to complete this book and the ideas needed to enrich and strengthen it. Thank you also to my former colleagues at the National Education Association for inspiring me to undertake this project.

Thank you to my research assistants, Linda Kim and Kay Fujiyoshi, for their volumes of background research and feedback. Thank you also to my friend and inspiration, Erica Meiners, and to my mentor, Carl Grant, for their generous suggestions and advice on earlier drafts.

I presented earlier versions of this research at various venues over the past couple of years, and I thank the many people who asked questions, encouraged me to continue, challenged me to clarify my thinking, and pointed me to additional resources.

Thank you to Carole Saltz of Teachers College Press for her unwavering support and vision, the many staff of TCP for their contributions and assistance, and the anonymous reviewers for their helpful and timely feedback.

I am honored to be a part of the Teaching for Social Justice book series, and I thank the editors, Bill Ayers and Therese Quinn, for their leadership. Thank you especially to Bill for the countless hours he devoted to giving suggestions, pushing me harder, and opening up the possibilities of this project.

Finally, I wish to thank the many people—educators, research-ers, leaders, activists—on whose work this book builds. Let us keep moving forward as we transform our schools and society into better places for all.

Introduction

For years, the kitchen cabinet in the house where I grew up displayed my self-portrait from 3rd grade. Below our portraits, we were to write what we wanted to be when we grew up. I wrote "Teacher." As far back as I can remember, I have wanted to be a teacher. I used to love seating together my "little people" toys with stuffed animals or chess pieces or whatever else I could find so that I had a big enough class to teach. I wanted to be a good teacher, which meant to me that I was to be strict. It just made "common sense" to me that being a good teacher meant being strict. As I grew older and taught daycare, and then elementary and middle school, and then high school, I tried hard to live up to the image that I developed early on, perhaps because I looked back to my own teachers and saw that those whom I thought were really good were those who, indeed, were strict. I hoped to have a similarly positive impact on my own students.

My teaching career took me from part-time jobs in college, to the Peace Corps in Nepal, to various schools in my hometown of Honolulu. As I moved from job to job, I would continue to visit the schools I had taught in previously. I remember one visit that was particularly sobering. I ran into a student, then a high school senior who had taken one of my math classes the year before. After remarking on how different I looked—because I was fatter and dressed like a slob—she asked if I knew how much she had hated my class. She laughed jokingly as she spoke, but there was truth behind her question. She may have liked me and thought that I was funny in a way that most of her teachers were not, and she may have liked some of the projects that we did in class, but she barely earned a C, reflecting her struggle throughout the year to learn. She knew that I was trying to help and she came in several times for tutoring, but she felt that I was not hearing her, that I was not understanding why she had such a hard time in class. As I thought about it, I realized that I had not really known why she struggled and, perhaps more important, that I had not taken the time to understand.

I went home that evening and obsessed about my former student's comments. I began thinking back to some of those teachers whom I liked best: my 5th-grade special education teacher, my middle school music teacher, my English teacher in my early high school years, and my foreign language teacher in my later high school years. Yes, they were strict. They demanded much in terms of how we behaved and what we produced. They made me want to learn. But they were also the teachers whom I felt knew something about me beyond the homework that I was turning in. It so happens that all of these teachers were ones who had me in classes for more than 1 year, and who also interacted with me in extracurricular activities in addition to the regular class times. Perhaps as a result, I felt that they took the time to learn more about me, including how I learned, why I struggled, what I cared about, and where I excelled. They then could take this information into account in the various aspects of teaching, from creating assignments and giving feedback in ways that addressed my weaknesses, to structuring group activities in ways that built on my strengths, to simply checking in once in a while and giving me a sign that I was being heard.

While growing up, I developed a whole set of values around being strict, being strong, being in control, and being demanding, particularly for adults in leadership roles, whether teachers, parents, or leaders in business and government. But I developed other values as well, including values about being nurturing, caring, connected, empathetic, and cooperative. My initial understanding of the "good teacher" was shaped, or *framed*, by the former set of values, and it was not until I was reminded of a whole other set of values that I held dear that I began to *reframe* and change my understanding of the "good teacher" and how I tried to embody it. George Lakoff (2004) explains framing and reframing as follows:

Frames are mental structures that shape the way we see the world. As a result, they shape the goals we seek, the plans we make, the way we act, and what counts as a good or bad outcome of our actions. In politics our frames shape our social policies and the institutions we form to carry out policies. To change our frames is to change all of this. Reframing *is* social change.

You can't see or hear frames. They are part of what cognitive scientists call the "cognitive unconscious"—structures in our brains that we cannot consciously access, but know by their consequences: the way we reason and what counts as common sense. We also know frames through language. All words are defined relative to conceptual frames. When you hear a word, its frame (or collection of frames) is activated in your brain.

Reframing is changing the way the public sees the world. It is changing what counts as common sense. (p. xv, emphasis in original)

So for me, changing what I took for granted as "common sense" required tapping into a different set of values that I already held but had not yet connected to teaching. I needed to reframe my understanding of good teaching.

"COMMON SENSE" AND SCHOOLING

What we take to be "common sense" is not something that just *is*; it is something that is developed and learned and perpetuated over time. I learned this when I headed to Nepal to begin work as a Peace Corps volunteer. In the village where I was stationed, there were many aspects of schooling that my neighbors seemed to take for granted as the ways schools are and should be, but that did not align with my own assumptions about schooling. For example, I wanted to seat students in mixed-gender groups, but learned that boys always sit together on one side of the room and girls on the other. The large number of students squeezed onto small benches made physical contact inevitable, which was fine among students of the same gender but culturally inappropriate otherwise. I tried to manage the classroom with dialogue and verbal admonitions, but often was told by the students and teachers that controlling the classroom meant hitting those who misbehaved. I risked being seen as lacking authority because I did not carry a stick.

Perhaps most significant, I wanted to introduce activities and materials and sample problems that I had created on my own, but was told that class lessons had always consisted of what was in the official textbooks—issued by the government, common to all schools, and the basis for the annual tests that determined whether students would move to the next grade level. "Common sense" dictated that teachers were to go over the solutions to the problems, which students were to copy down and memorize, primarily because the high-stakes exams consisted of these very problems. By not doing what was expected, and by presumably jeopardizing their chances of passing the exams, I was confronted with criticism by students who complained not merely that I was not teaching well, but that I was not teaching at all. What I was doing did not make sense.

As is the case in Nepal, many aspects of schooling in the United States have become so routine and commonplace that they often go unquestioned. Across the nation and for both young children and adolescents, schools generally open from early morning until midafternoon, Monday through Friday, from the end of summer until the beginning of the next summer. Students spend most of their time studying the four "core disciplines" of reading, mathematics, social studies, and the natural sciences, and, less frequently, foreign languages, the arts, physical education, and vocational education. Classes in each subject generally last between 1 and 2 hours, meet every day or every other day, and consist of one teacher, perhaps an adult assistant, and a group of about 10, 20, 30, maybe 40 students. Students usually are grouped by age, sometimes by gender, and often by ability. Teaching and learning usually take place in a four-walled room where students sit for most of the period, working out of shared books or writing on shared topics or engaging in shared experiments. Teachers are expected to know more than the students, determine what students are supposed to learn, structure the class in such a way that students learn what they are supposed to learn, and then assess whether they learned it, with exams or assignments. Students are expected to follow instructions, work hard, and do homework in order to learn what they are supposed to, and the grade, score, or rank with which they end up is meant to reflect the degree to which they succeeded. Framed as common sense in education, this is what many people take to be what "real" schools look like.

Throughout history, schools have taken on a variety of forms, and even today some schools design alternative ways to schedule classes, organize the curriculum, and group students, as well as alternative types of activities, assessments, and goals. Yet, over the past century, the commonsense view of schools has persisted, and has hindered attempts to change aspects of schooling that often are taken to be fundamental, including how students are grouped, how subjects are divided, and how learning is assessed (Tyack & Tobin, 1994). Attempts to improve schooling that defy "common sense" have been dismissed as biased or politically motivated, as a distraction from the real work of schools, as inappropriate for children, or simply as nonsensical, particularly when the reforms call attention to such hot-button, controversial issues as racism, sexism, poverty, and the ways that schools can reinforce them.

"Common sense" narrowly defines what is considered to be consistent with the purposes of schooling. Common sense does not tell us that this is what schools *could* be doing; it tells us that this and only this is what schools *should* be doing. To reform schools in a fundamental way, one first must redefine common sense and reframe how we think about education.

"RIGHT," "LEFT," AND PUBLIC EDUCATION

One way to understand the various reforms in education is to contrast the efforts of those who want to maintain the status quo, particularly its hierarchies and privileges, with the efforts of those who want to change the status quo by raising awareness of and challenging the racism, sexism, and other forms of oppression that permeate schools and society. The former is led by the political Right in the United States; the latter, by the Left.

These groups are difficult to identify by constituent or issue, which have changed over time. Today, for example, conservatives and Republicans often are identified with the Right, and liberals and progressives with the Left. However, a brief look back in history reveals that the Democrats in the mid-1900s, particularly the Southern Democrats, were identified with the Right because of their active defense of White supremacy and racial segregation. The Democrats in the 1990s, particularly the "New" Democrats led by President Bill Clinton, were identified with the center, disliked by some on the Left because of their pro-business policies. Recently, some groups that traditionally have been identified as leaders of the Left have been criticized for supporting the Right, as when such education and labor organizations as the American Federation of Teachers and the National Education Association failed, in the minds of many educators, to challenge the education policies stemming from the conservative Reagan Administration and continuing through the 2001 No Child Left Behind Act. Policy initiatives have varied similarly, with differences of opinion within the Right and within the Left, and coalitions have formed that consist of groups from both the Right and the Left on such issues as charter schools, hate-crimes legislation, immigration, Israel and the Middle East, same-sex marriage, and welfare reform.

What defines and differentiates the Right and the Left are not their constituents or issues, which can differ at any given time, but their underlying goals: The Left aims to change the status quo and the Right aims to maintain it. For the Right, this goal is often manifested in initiatives to undermine those public institutions that can have the most impact in changing the status quo, such as the government, social welfare services, and, of course, the public education system. Public education, after all, is seen by many Americans to be what philosopher Horace Mann called "the great equalizer of the conditions of men," as that which can rectify the unequal conditions in society and give every person a chance for prosperity. That is, public education has the potential to change the very conditions that historically have benefited certain groups. It is not surprising, then, that in recent years the Right has launched a series of policy initiatives that aim to undermine public education.

Increasingly, the Right has been successful in finding support from both major political parties, as well as the American public, for its initiatives. The reason? Because the Right is successfully reframing common sense in education.

This book examines the power of frames to influence public opinion and advance policy agendas, particularly the frames used by the Right to undermine public education and reinforce inequities regarding social class, gender and sexuality, and race. Chapter 1 paints a landscape of the Right, including its history, major players, policy priorities, and strategies, and details five current policy priorities within education: tax cuts and privatization, funding and spending restrictions, alternative teacher certification, censorship, and standards and testing. Chapter 2 describes how four primary framings from the Right—"traditional family," "free enterprise," "beacon of goodness," and "be very afraid"—are able to tap into core values of the American public, redefine common sense, mask our own imperialism, and intersect with and reinforce one another as they influence public opinion. Chapters 3 and 4 examine in detail two initiatives from the Right—institutionalizing bias regarding gender and sexuality, and assimilating racial difference—to reveal the Right's strategic use and appropriation of frames, as well as the Left's failure to reframe the problem. Lastly, Chapter 5 imagines frames that hold promise for a broader coalition on the Left to reform education in ways that truly make schools and society better places for all.

CHAPTER 1

Attack on Public Education

One of the most important objects of the rightist agendas is changing our common-sense, altering the meanings of the most basic categories, the key words, we employ to understand the social and educational world and our place in it.

—Michael Apple, 2001, p. 9

The Right is difficult to characterize because it consists of groups vastly divergent ideologically and politically. According to Michael Apple (2001), in the field of education today the Right consists of four not always coherent groups: neoliberals who believe in the value of competitive markets and the freedom of individual choice; neoconservatives who believe that things were better in the past and want to return to traditional notions of discipline and knowledge; authoritarian populists, including the Christian Right, who believe that God should be in all institutions; and a particular segment of the managerial and professional middle class who believe in the value of centralized control and advocate for more rigorous standards and tests. Speaking of the Right in broader U.S. society, Kathleen deMarrais (2006) delineates an even longer list: the Christian Right, conservative internationalists, the conservative mainstream, libertarians, militant anticommunists, national security militarists, neoconservatives, the new Right, the old-guard Right, paleoconservatives, and social conservatives. The Leftist think tank Political Research Associates (http://www.publiceye.org) categorizes many of these groups into three primary submovements, as illustrated in Figure 1.1. The *secular Right* includes business nationalists, corporate internationalists, economic libertarians, national security militarists, and neoconservatives, and aims to preserve economic privilege. The *Christian Right* includes Christian nationalists and theocrats, and aims primarily to uphold traditional notions of gender and sexuality. The *xenophobic Right* includes the extreme Right, paleoconservatives, patriots, and White nationalists, and aims to protect the privileges of certain racial groups and nations, often under the guise of protecting borders.

Historically, "the Right" emerged as the result of various groups coalescing for a common purpose and against a common enemy. The purpose was to challenge the legal and cultural changes regarding race, social class, gender, and other social markers that were brought about by the civil rights movements in the 1950s and 1960s. The enemy, at least early on, was the "liberal establishment," which steered and supported these movements. That was how it was in 1971 when an internal memo of the U.S. Chamber of Commerce, known as the Powell Manifesto (penned by Lewis Powell, who soon after became an Associate Justice on the U.S. Supreme Court), articulated this common enemy and purpose in its description of a concerted Leftist attack on the so-called American "free enterprise" system (i.e., the U.S. political economy) and on American democracy itself, and the resulting need to act. In response to the Powell Manifesto, a group of conservatives, particularly philanthropists with family business fortunes,

FIGURE 1.1. Primary Submovements of the Right

Secular	R	⟶	*Preserve economic privilege*
	I		
Christian	G	⟶	*Uphold traditional notions of gender and sexuality*
	H		
Xenophobic	T	⟶	*Protect the privileges of certain racial groups and nations*

came together and formed a Philanthropy Roundtable that would strategize about how to use their funding for building a Rightist movement.

In the decades to follow, Rightist philanthropists developed four interconnected funding priorities or strategies to advance public policy agendas that were pro-business and anti-social welfare, in other words, that would enable the U.S. political and economic system to continue to benefit certain groups in society. The priority was to develop four programs: a cadre of students in higher education who would embrace Rightist ideologies; a generation of scholars who would produce research that made Rightist ideologies accessible and who would then enter government service; a network of Rightist regional and state policy think tanks and advocacy organizations; and a protocol for using media to reach the public effectively (deMarrais, 2006). Their strategies have been quite successful, as evidenced by the emergence of education and government leaders (e.g., Dinesh D'Souza, Chester Finn, Newt Gingrich, Diane Ravitch, and Thomas Sowell) who were beneficiaries of the philanthropists' fellowships and other forms of professional support, and evidenced as well by the increase in the media and legislation of Rightist ideologies that were developed in their think tanks.

Perhaps the most notable difference between Rightist and Leftist philanthropic organizations is the expectation placed on how the organizations will use their funds. Whereas the Left tends to fund a large number of organizations for specific projects of limited term and scope, the Right funds the general operations of a smaller number of organizations over longer periods of time in order to build institutional infrastructure (Krehely, House, & Kernan, 2004). The Right especially targets funding to organizations that aggressively lobby in state legislatures and Congress, and that engage effectively in media campaigns, thus ensuring that Rightist ideas are enacted into law with public support. Consequently, the Right has emerged as an interconnected web of organizations with aligned missions and coordinated strategies, often facilitated by shared board members.

ORGANIZATIONAL LANDSCAPE OF THE RIGHT

Media Transparency (http://www.mediatransparency.org) and People for the American Way (http://www.pfaw.org) are Leftist organizations that track the various organizations in the Right and critically analyze their strategies and initiatives. They have identified four general categories of Rightist organizations: foundations, think tanks, advocacy organizations, and political action committees. Of course, there is much overlap and some organizations fit multiple categories, but the various types of organizations are responsible for unique roles, as illustrated in Figure 1.2.

Foundations (and wealthy individuals and families) are the philanthropic entities that fund and, consequently, shape the work of the Right. Until recently the four most influential were Bradley, Olin, Scaife, and Smith Richardson, known as the Four Sisters. The Lynde and Harry Bradley Foundation in Wisconsin is, according to Media Transparency, the country's largest and most influential Rightist foundation, and includes among its priorities the dismantling of affirmative action and of welfare. William Bennett, Secretary of Education under President Reagan, is a former board member, and perhaps not surprising, Bradley is involved in education policy initiatives as well, including the support of school voucher programs and privatization. The John M. Olin Foundation, ceased as of 2005, focused on developing research through

FIGURE 1.2. Organizational Landscape of the Right

think tanks and universities, making large gifts to Harvard, Yale, the University of Chicago, and other universities, as well as to individual researchers. The Scaife Family Foundations (consisting of the Sarah Scaife, Allegheny, and Carthage Foundations), funded by the Mellon family fortune, gives to a range of think tanks and lobbying and publishing groups. The H. Smith Richardson Foundation in North Carolina supports, in its own words, the "next generation of public policy researchers and analysts" by funding think tanks and universities. Notably, several think tanks have received funding from all four Sisters, including the American Enterprise Institute for Public Policy, Heritage Foundation, and Hoover Institution. According to deMarrais,

> This deliberate, focused, and substantial funding over many years given to a small number of conservative think tanks has enabled those institutes to grow in their capacity to produce "scholarship" that is fed in the form of highly accessible research and policy briefs to the media as well as federal and state legislators to shape the dialogue, and then support and promote policies around particular issues *with education at the top of the list.* (2006, p. 216, emphasis added)

Media Transparency identifies several other foundations that gave over $100 million to Rightist causes between 1998 and 2004, including Walton and DeVos. The Walton Family Foundation in Arkansas (created by the heirs to Sam Walton of Wal-Mart, the world's largest corporation) is the most influential foundation in promoting school vouchers and has financed nearly every ballot initiative for vouchers since 1993. Walton funds such provoucher organizations as the Alliance for School Choice, as well as organizations that draw communities of color into the provoucher movement, such as the Black Alliance for Educational Options and the Hispanic Council for Reform and Educational Options. The Richard and Helen DeVos Foundation in Michigan, funded by the AmWay fortune, supports vouchers as well as organizations of the Christian Right, including Focus on the Family. Another notable foundation is the Castle Rock Foundation in Colorado, endowed by the Coors Foundation, which supports vouchers and opposes organized labor. While not a private foundation, it should be noted that the current Bush Administration also has contributed significant financial support to Rightist organizations, particularly for vouchers, privatization, and alternative teacher certification.

Think tanks are national and state-level organizations, funded primarily by the foundations, that produce the research and media messages needed to support policy change. Arguably the most prominent is the national Heritage Foundation, founded by philanthropists Joseph Coors, Richard Mellon Scaife, and others. Heritage often is considered a model and source of research for the state-level think tanks, particularly regarding school vouchers and privatization. Other national think tanks include the American Enterprise Institute for Public Policy, Cato Institute, Center for Education Reform, and Hoover Institution. At the state level are think tanks like the 50-member State Policy Network that give a "local" voice to issues despite the fact that they often are funded and supported by national foundations and think tanks. Like the national think tanks, state-level think tanks are not-for-profit organizations (501(c)3, according to the Internal Revenue Service) and, as such, are prohibited by law from lobbying for legislation or candidates for office. However, also like their national counterparts, they focus on influencing legislation and candidates indirectly through research, polling data, media campaigns, conferences and educational events, and "expert" testimonies before legislative bodies, particularly regarding tax and education policies. Active and influential state-level think tanks include the Evergreen Freedom Foundation in Olympia (WA), Heartland Institute in Chicago, Independence Institute in Golden (CO), Manhattan Institute in New York City, and Reason Foundation in Los Angeles.

Advocacy organizations do the work of community organizing, public relations, programming, and otherwise generating public support for the policy initiatives that were articulated by the foundations and supported with research and messages by the think tanks. Funding for advocacy organizations comes from foundations as well as corporations. These organizations include provoucher organizations like the Alliance for School Choice, as well as organizations that critique the media and academia for being "too liberal," such as Accuracy in Academia (and its sister, Accuracy in Media), funded by the Scaife Family Foundations, which monitors and publicly criticizes professors who are believed to be indoctrinating their students with Leftist ideology. Advocacy organizations also include professional organizations that were created to counter the two prominent labor organizations in education—the American Federation of Teachers and the National Education Association; while some originally were not self-identified with the Right, they have come to receive funding from Rightist foundations and, in turn, to align their messages and strategies with the Right. Examples include the Association of American Educators (http://www.aaeteachers.org), Christian Educators Association International (http://www.ceai.org), and a growing number of state-level organizations. Some advocacy organizations identify with the Christian Right, including Focus on the Family, the largest evangelical Christian organization in the United States, and Concerned Women for America, which has focused its efforts in recent years on opposing abortion, comprehensive sex education, and gay rights. One particularly important advocacy organization is the American Legislative Exchange Council, a network of legislators and advisors that drafts model legislation for implementing Rightist agendas.

Political action committees (PACs) often work hand-in-hand with advocacy organizations, but they are 501(c)4 organizations (not 501(c)3) and, as such, are legally allowed to lobby for legislation, ballot initiatives, and candidates running for office. Examples of PACs include the All Children Matter PAC, Americans for Prosperity Foundation, Americans for Tax Reform, CSE Freedom-Works, Club for Growth, Legislative Education Action Drive, and Republican State Leadership Committee. The impact of the PACs in consort with the other types of organizations has been profound as the Right increasingly shapes public opinion, education policy, and even federal legislation, translating the priorities of its three primary submovements (namely, the secular, Christian, and xenophobic Right) into policy change.

CURRENT INITIATIVES TO
UNDERMINE PUBLIC EDUCATION

Tax Cuts and Privatization

Given the Right's emergence in response to a perceived Leftist attack on "free enterprise," it is not surprising that one of the shared priorities across the various Rightist organizations is that of dismantling any aspect of government that reflects a welfare state, particularly such big-budget items as health care and education. Primarily, this takes two forms: reducing the amount of taxes that the government collects and redistributes in the form of public services (cutting taxes), and restructuring whatever services are being provided into a market-like industry (privatizing).

Cutting taxes remains a policy priority for the Right, particularly in the form of "tax and expenditure limitations," which restrict revenue growth via either legislation or referendum. At the state level, perhaps the most severe form of this limitation is the so-called Taxpayers Bill of Rights (TABOR), a state constitutional amendment that would restrict revenue or expenditure growth to the sum of inflation plus population change, require voter approval to override the revenue or spending limits, and promise tax refunds to taxpayers of any revenues deemed to be "excess." The rationale seems reasonable: The government's income and expenses should not grow at a faster rate than those of families. But the problem is that the costs of the programs and services on which the government spends most of its money, particularly healthcare and education, are rising much faster than the general rate of inflation. According to the national Center on Budget and Policy Priorities (http://www.cbpp.org/ssl-series.htm), TABOR would result in not merely slowing the growth of state budgets, but shrinking them. Services like healthcare and education, the very services most utilized by the least advantaged in society, would be hardest hit proportionally. Colorado is the only state to have passed a TABOR, back in 1992, and since then it has experienced drastic declines in K–12 spending, higher education spending, and health insurance for children. In 2005, Colorado voters suspended TABOR for 5 years to try to begin restoring cut services. Nonetheless, year after year, the Right continues to advocate for TABOR and other limitations, and although TABOR has not found support by voters in any other states' referenda, other forms of tax and expenditure limitations have been approved by legislatures in a majority of states.

Privatizing occurs when public services are restructured into a market-like industry, thus shifting funds, oversight, and accountability from the government to individuals and/or corporations (Duggan, 2003). Within education, the Right leads at least two initiatives toward privatization: school vouchers and outsourcing. School vouchers apply public tax dollars toward tuition for private schools, including parochial schools, resulting in less funding for public education. According to the Progressive States Network (http://www.progressivestates.org), a research and advocacy organization that aims to advance Leftist policy change at the state level, the Right led 12 state ballot initiatives from 1970 to 2000 on vouchers and tax credits, all of which the public rejected with a cumulative 68% to 32% margin. Yet the initiatives have continued, and according to the National Education Association the Right spends $65 million annually on voucher initiatives. In 2005, following the devastation left in the wake of Hurricane Katrina, the Bush Administration proposed legislation for "Katrina vouchers," which was to provide some funds for the 300,000 students displaced by Katrina to attend private schools. Co-sponsored by one of the more liberal Democrats, Senator Edward Kennedy, the bill was approved by Congress as the Hurricane Education Recovery Act (Title IV of the 2005 Defense Appropriations Act). The "Katrina vouchers" were extended in 2006, and the Left is bracing for voucher battles to intensify in courts and in state legislatures, especially as the voucher debate becomes reframed from an issue of "freedom of choice" (whereby all parents should have the freedom to choose where to send their children to school, and should be provided with the means to do so) to a seemingly more compassionate issue of "support for those in dire need."

Outsourcing is the hiring of private companies to provide services and goods. Private schools are not the only entities to benefit from privatization. More and more "virtual schools" are emerging to manage the curriculum for children who are being homeschooled. According to the Progressive States Network, roughly half the states have created some version of virtual schools, and others are considering legislation that would support them. The companies that run these virtual schools benefit from tax dollars. One example is K12, Inc., co-founded by William Bennett, which, according to the federal Government Accountability Office, has improperly received millions of federal grant dollars from the U.S. Department of Education. Private companies also are being hired to manage charter schools, regular public schools, and entire school districts, such as the Edison Project, which currently manages schools and school districts in 19 states and the District of Columbia. All together, more than 50 such for-profit "education management organizations" currently are managing roughly 460 schools in 28 states and the District of Columbia.

A rapidly growing number of private companies also are being hired to provide textbooks, vending machines, cleaning and office supplies, transportation and food services, substitute teachers, and, of course, services and materials related to standardized testing and reporting. There is much profit to be made in public education: Nearly $400 billion is spent on K–12 public education annually. Even the Bush family is profiting from this market: Brother Neil Bush is founder and CEO of Ignite! Inc., which has earned tens of millions of dollars selling software that helps students prepare for taking standardized tests (Wheeler, 2003). The federal No Child Left Behind (NCLB) Act facilitates privatization in its "supplemental education services" provision in Title I, which requires schools that are not making "annual yearly progress" for 2 years to provide after-school tutoring, opening what is potentially a $2 billion market. Significantly, this provision does not place upon the service providers some of the requirements that school districts would face if they provided the tutoring themselves, such as access to services for students with special needs. And, NCLB does not provide funding to schools that are required to provide tutoring, leaving it up to the districts to find the funds.

Funding and Spending Restrictions

Overall, the federal government has underfunded NCLB by tens of billions of dollars since its inception in 2002, according to one of the leading critics of NCLB, the National Education Association (http://www.nea.org). As organizations like NEA call for more funding for public education, other organizations counter that the problem is not the amount of funding but the ways in which that funding gets used.

One such organization, First Class Education, argues that too much of current school district budgets is spent on administrative costs. Improving schools, it argues, requires increasing the amount spent on the part of schooling that reaches students directly, namely, classroom instruction. First Class Education prioritizes what the National Center for Education Statistics calls "classroom instruction" or "in the classroom" spending, which primarily includes teacher and aide salaries and instruction supplies. On its website (http://www.firstclasseducation.org) First Class Education makes two arguments. First, overall education funding nationwide has increased while the percentage of school district budgets that was spent on "classroom instruction" has decreased. Currently, less than 62% of budgets is spent on "classroom instruction." Second, increasing the spending to 65% would result in billions more per year ($14 billion in 2002–2003, for example) spent on "classroom instruction" (without any increase in taxes), which is important because classroom instruction is the part of schooling that they argue is most likely to raise student achievement, as measured by standardized test scores. This is the "65% Solution."

Research does not support this "solution." According to a study released by Standard & Poor's (2005), there is "no significant positive correlation between the percentage of funds that districts spend on instruction and the percentage of students who score proficient or higher on state reading and math tests," which means that districts spending over 65% on "classroom instruction" were not more likely to see higher test scores. Increasing the percentage spent "in the classroom" has not been proven to raise student achievement. This should not be surprising. What gets defined as "outside" the classroom includes some of the very services that target the students in most need. Reallocating funds to increase "classroom instruction" requires cutting not only administrative services but also student services like health, nursing and counseling, curriculum development and teacher training, libraries, facilities and maintenance, food services, and transportation. By increasing the percentage spent "in the classroom," less money is left for what remains outside. No new money is being added.

First Class Education's goal is for all 50 states and the District of Columbia to pass laws requiring school districts to spend at least 65% of operating budgets on "classroom instruction" by 2008. By the summer of 2007, four states had passed some form of the "65% Solution": Georgia passed a law, Kansas passed a "public policy goal," the governor of Texas issued an executive order, and the Louisiana legislature passed a nonbinding resolution. Legislation and/or ballot initiatives are expected or already underway in Arizona, Colorado, Florida, Illinois, Michigan, Minnesota, Missouri, Ohio, Oklahoma, Oregon, and Washington state. The outlook is good for First Class Education because the "65% Solution" polls well among the general public: The nonpartisan Harris Polling found support to be between 70% and 80% (Carr, 2006). This initiative even has bipartisan support, including from Democratic governor Bill Richardson of New Mexico.

Arguably, the appeal of the "65% Solution" lies in its framing. The language of "waste" and "classroom instruction" taps into sensibilities that many people can relate to. Many of us can think of examples of waste in schools, organizations, businesses, governments, even households, and how we would spend that money better or more efficiently or fairly. Many of us can think of examples of bloated bureaucracies that get in the way of teachers doing what they are supposed to be doing, namely, teaching. In other words, the "65% Solution" can seem reasonable if we agree that there is much waste and that the first step to improving schools is spending existing funds more effectively. This is important in order to counter groups like NEA that are calling for more education funding, as well as to appease the public when Congress actually is cutting funding, as happened in December 2005 when the Defense Appropriations Act (the same Act that authorized the "Katrina vouchers") resulted in 1% across-the-board cuts and additional cuts to targeted programs, totaling over $1 billion less for education. Perhaps not surprising, leaders of First Class Education have ties to initiatives and organizations pushing for tax cuts and privatization, including Republican political consultant Tim Mooney and Overstock.com CEO Patrick Byrne, who has privately financed much of this initiative.

Alternative Teacher Certification

A leading advocate for the privatization of schools is Chester Finn, co-founder of the education management organization Edison Project and current president of the Thomas B. Fordham Foundation (and who, incidentally, is one of the few Rightist leaders who has spoken out against the "65% Solution"; see Phillips, 2006). A former assistant secretary in the U.S. Department of Education during the Reagan Administration, Finn has maintained close ties with that administration, as evidenced by his ongoing work and publications with then-Secretary of Education William Bennett. Soon after the second President Bush entered office, the U.S. Department of Education granted $5 million, half of which was unsolicited, for the creation of the American Board for Certification of Teacher Excellence (U.S. Department of Education Grant Award Database, http://www. bcol02.ed.gov/cfapps/grantaward/start.cfm), for which Finn has served as executive director. Two years later, the Department of Education gave ABCTE an additional $35 million multi-year grant to create a fast-track alternative route to teacher certification. The Department of Education remains the primary funding source for ABCTE (and Chester Finn remains an advisor on education policy to President Bush).

Called the "Passport to Teaching," ABCTE's fast-track program awards initial teacher certification based primarily on knowledge of subject matter to be taught. Candidates must hold a bachelor's degree and either have majored in the subject to be taught or have taken a sufficient number of courses in that subject, and must pass examinations of the subject area and of "teaching knowledge" that can take the form of online, standardized tests. Candidates never need to take courses on, say, how inequities play out in schools, how different students learn, how to design curriculum, or how policies and social contexts impact teaching and learning, nor are they required to participate in any field experience. Upon paying a fee and passing a federal background check, candidates are eligible for initial certification in states that accept the "Passport."

Initially, ABCTE had success in getting state credentialing agencies to accept the "Passport" as an alternative route to initial certification for public school teaching. Pennsylvania began accepting the "Passport" in 2002; Idaho in 2003; Florida, New Hampshire, and Utah (for secondary mathematics) in 2004. In 2004, ABCTE approached the California Commission on Teacher Credentialing, and that summer, as the Commission's hearing on ABCTE approached, a growing number of teacher educators expressed fears that acceptance of the "Passport" by California could lead to many other states following suit. Teacher educators in the Alliance for Progressive Teacher Education in California (http://antioppressiveeducation.org/aptec.html) joined with other community and advocacy organizations to write letters to newspapers, meet with lawmakers, and testify at the Commission's hearing and attend in large numbers.

The organizing worked, and the Commission decided against accepting the "Passport," but the success was bittersweet. The large number of university faculty members speaking out against ABCTE raised concerns among some community members who, in personal conversations with me, said that they felt that the faculty members were being hypocritical. On the one hand, the faculty members were arguing that high-quality teachers not only have learned the subject matter, but also have learned how to teach, which does not happen in the "Passport to Teaching" program. But on the other hand, faculties in higher education, including those in teacher preparation programs, are teaching in a profession that does not require, in order to be hired, learning how to teach, and in fact often bases decisions about hiring and promotion solely on knowledge and expertise in the subject matter. Higher education, in other words, was considered by some to be framed by the very definition of teacher quality that the faculties were fighting against, raising questions about why ABCTE was a target of criticism, but not higher education itself. ABCTE did not gain more states for the "Passport" in 2005, but in 2007 ABCTE's website (http://www.abcte.org) claimed that it offered the "Passport" as an alternative route to state certification in two additional states—South Carolina and Mississippi—as well as certification for charter schools in Arizona, the District of Columbia, and Texas and for private schools in all 50 states. The demand for the "Passport" may increase as ABCTE launches Project 5000, an ongoing initiative to certify via the "Passport" 5,000 new math and science teachers by 2008, recruited from math and science professionals who are interested in a fast track to entering the teaching profession.

In addition, ABCTE piloted a second certification program in 2007, namely the Master Teacher Certificate program. As an alternative to certification by the National Board for Professional Teaching Standards, but at half the cost, ABCTE's Master Teacher Certificate is like the "Passport" in that it requires knowledge of subject matter as demonstrated on standardized exams, but additionally it requires one indication of teaching efficacy, namely that student test scores have gone up over time. This Master Teacher Certificate has the potential to gain popularity and acceptance across the country for several reasons. First, pursuing the certificate is half as costly and much less time-consuming than pursuing National Board certification. Second, accepting the certificate for promotion or salary increases is a decision made at the district or school level, not the state level, making it more difficult for critics of ABCTE to monitor, much less challenge, its acceptance and use. Third, and perhaps most important, defining teacher quality in terms of content knowledge and raised test scores taps into common and commonsense ways of thinking about what it means to be a good teacher.

Taken together, the "65% Solution" and ABCTE's certificates mean less funding for schools and less preparation of teachers. Yet both initiatives are finding public and political support. The Right has been successful at reframing the very ways that we think about efficiency, about teacher quality, and so on, or perhaps more accurately, it has been successful at altering the very ways that we understand what makes for "common sense." Its initiative on censorship in higher education is illustrative.

Censorship

Over the past few years, particularly following September 11, 2001, the Right has launched a series of initiatives to silence certain perspectives in the academy. This has happened at the national, state, and campus levels. For example, at the national level in 2003 (HR 3077) and again in 2005 (HR 509), Congress considered legislation to increase government's monitoring of and influence over international studies in higher education. Spurred in part by the Left's growing criticism of post–9/11 U.S. foreign policies and military involvement, the Right argued that international education should support the work of government, not hinder it. As explained by Stanley Kurtz of the Rightist Hudson Institute, international education should promote not only an understanding of the rest of the world, but also a particular (i.e., laudatory) understanding of the relationship of the United States to the rest of the world (Prashad, 2006). The implication here is that Leftists are threatening national security when they critique the Bush Administration. Such was the argument by the American Council of Trustees and Alumni (http://www.goacta.org), which named and criticized professors who spoke out against the Bush Administration's war policies, and which includes among its co-founders Lynne Cheney, wife of Vice President Dick Cheney, and Senator Joseph Lieberman of Connecticut. Echoing these arguments were Americans for Victory Over Terrorism (http://www.avot.org), whose co-founders include William Bennett, and Campus Watch (http://www.campus-watch.org), founded by Daniel Pipes, who was appointed by the current President Bush to the U.S. Institute of Peace, despite opposition from Democrats to his pro-war stance (Aziz, 2004).

The Right's attack on professors is not limited to those in international studies. The Rightist think tank Pacific Research Institute (which is funded largely by Scaife and, previously, Olin) has been a leader in attacking scholars in labor studies (Aziz, 2004). A field once focused on fostering labor–management cooperation and preventing struggle, labor studies today focuses primarily on the oppression and empowerment of the working classes, and thus is often critical of corporate practices and of the capitalist economic system overall.

Leftists are taking over higher education, according to the Rightist advocacy organization Accuracy in Academia as well as David Horowitz, founder and president of the Rightist think tank Center for the Study of Popular Culture and author of the 2006 book *The Professors: The 101 Most Dangerous Academics in America*, which profiles professors whom he claims are harming education with Leftist propaganda. A few years prior to the book, Horowitz founded the advocacy network Students for Academic Freedom in order to support students in monitoring and exposing professors like these. In the years since, chapters have sprung up on campuses across the country, and private and public criticism and condemnation have increased, as have governmental surveillance and loss of job security (Younge, 2006). In tandem with Students for Academic Freedom is the initiative, also led by Horowitz, to get more states and universities to adopt a so-called Academic Bill of Rights, either through legislation, policy, or resolution. The bill states that "academic freedom is most likely to thrive in an environment of intellectual diversity," and furthermore that "intellectual independence means the protection of students—as well as faculty—from the imposition of any orthodoxy of a political, religious, or ideological nature" (http://www.studentsforacademicfreedom.org/abor.html). According to Free Exchange on Campus (http://www.freeexchangeoncampus.org), which is a coalition of organizations opposed to censorship in higher education, the bill is misleading. When the bill speaks of "intellectual diversity," it really seeks to increase the number of conservatives in order to balance the supposed preponderance of liberals. When the bill speaks of "protection from imposition of any orthodoxy," it really seeks to silence liberals who purportedly are indoctrinating students. Strategically, a bill that is intended to limit free speech (of liberals) is framed by language of academic freedom and diversity.

The initiatives have not been altogether successful as measured by legislation. As of the summer of 2007, legislatures in roughly half of the states have considered such a bill of rights, but only two states (Georgia and Pennsylvania) have passed related resolutions, while three others (Colorado, Ohio, and Tennessee) have agreements with public college and university presidents to monitor their own institutions. In Congress, House Republicans included a provision for "intellectual diversity" in public colleges and universities in the 2005 and 2006 proposed reauthorizations of the Higher Education Act (HR 609). Legislative success, however, does not seem to be Horowitz's overall goal. According to Horowitz, "The aim of the movement isn't really to achieve legislation. . . . It's supposed to act as a cattle prod, to make legislators and universities more aware . . . [that] you can't get hired if you're a conservative in American universities" (as quoted in Younge, 2006). In fact, according to Horowitz, the Academic Bill of Rights does not need to win in legislatures for this initiative to be successful, as long as the public comes to share the underlying assumption that Leftists have indeed taken over the academy.

To date, the empirical research is inconclusive regarding this supposed liberal bias in the academy. For example, Horowitz's own study (Horowitz & Lehrer, n.d.) looked at only "elite" colleges and universities and found that a vast majority voted as Democratic versus Republican. Assuming that Democratic means liberal, that a majority-Democratic faculty necessarily will impose liberal ideology on campus climate and classroom instruction, and that the sample colleges were representative, the study found a significant liberal bias in higher education. A similar study (Klein & Stern, 2004) looked at voting records for only social science and humanities professors, and without looking at other disciplines or even other factors in determining campus and classroom climate, reached a similar conclusion. Even if a majority of professors self-identified on the Left, their larger numbers would need to be balanced with the policies, cultures, curriculums, and other aspects of education that researchers have long argued to be oppressive (Kumashiro, 2002), thus making their numbers merely one of many factors in shaping the "bias" of any educational context.

Nonetheless, the Right seems to be winning this battle over public opinion. As I began speaking across the United States about the Academic Bill of Rights, I commonly was asked why this was a problem, given that the academy "really is" more Leftist, as some would say. Even among self-identified Leftists, a perception that the academy is in fact more Leftist than Rightist seems to prevail. This is not unlike public perceptions of the media, which often seem to take for granted the notion that the media has a liberal bent, despite a growing field of critical media studies that reveals otherwise (see, for example, Macedo & Steinberg, 2007). Debates seem more focused on how to address this liberal bias, rather than on whether there really is such a bias, and whose or what purposes it serves when we fail to question the assumption that such a bias exists. Perhaps this is why Horowitz seems less concerned about immediate legislative success: When even the Left comes to use the language of the Right, certain assumptions or goals can remain unquestioned.

Standards and Testing

In January 2002, President Bush signed into law the No Child Left Behind Act, which reauthorized the Elementary and Secondary Education Act (ESEA) and instituted changes that both Democrats and Republicans were calling the most substantial since the law's creation in 1965 (Rudalevige, 2003). Although credited to the Bush Administration, NCLB had wide bipartisan support and was co-sponsored by one of the more senior and liberal members of the Democratic Party, Senator Edward Kennedy.

Of course, NCLB did not originate with the Bush Administration. Much of the framework for NCLB was developed in the final years of the Clinton Administration under Democratic appointees and staff.

Although some of the details of NCLB changed with the change of administration, several central concepts or frames remained intact. In fact, in the presidential campaigns of subsequent Democratic candidates (Al Gore in 2000 and John Kerry in 2004), the public heard proposals that may have differed from NCLB in the details, but that remained within four central frames:

- *Standards*: We need to have high standards for students, teachers, and schools.
- *Accountability*: We need to hold students, teachers, and schools accountable for reaching those standards and demonstrating that they did so on such measures as standardized tests.
- *Sanctions*: There will be sanctions for not meeting those standards and rewards for doing so.
- *Choice*: In those schools that do not meet standards, parents should have the choice to move their children elsewhere.

These frames, especially regarding standards and testing, trace back to even before the Clinton Administration. Although the 1994 reauthorization of ESEA during the Clinton Administration required states to develop content and performance standards and created the notion of "adequate yearly progress," the Rightist think tank Hoover Institution argues that NCLB culminates a standards-and-testing movement that began in 1983 when the Reagan Administration released the report *A Nation at Risk* (Rudalevige, 2003). Education reform has been framed by the language of standards and testing for over 2 decades from both political parties as well as in individual school districts across the nation. The Chicago Public School District, for example, influenced Clinton's vision of education reform by providing what he called "a model for the nation" in its use of standards, high-stakes testing, school accountability, and centralized regulation of teachers and schools (Lipman, 2004). From both Republicans and Democrats, proposals for education reform remained within the same frames, reinforcing the notion that these frames are given, taken-for-granted, merely "common sense."

The four frames are tightly linked to one another, which helps to expose how the standards-and-testing movement propels the public school system toward privatization. As Lakoff (2004) explains:

> Why an education bill about school testing? Once the testing frame applies not just to students but also to *schools*, then schools can, metaphorically, fail—and be punished for failing by having their allowance cut. Less funding in turn makes it harder for the schools to improve, which leads to a cycle of failure and ultimately elimination for many public schools. What replaces the public school system is a voucher system to support private schools. The wealthy would have good schools—paid for in part by what used to be tax payments for public schools. The poor would not have the money for good schools. We would wind up with a two-tier school system, a good one for the "deserving rich" and a bad one for the "undeserving poor." (p. 32, emphasis in original)

That is, the movement toward standards and testing goes hand-in-hand with the movements toward privatization, spending restrictions, and other policies from the Right. The attack on public education is a long-term, multifaceted one with various initiatives that intersect one another.

CONTRADICTIONS AND STRANGE BEDFELLOWS

A number of contradictions arise in the initiatives from the Right. For example, the push to produce teachers who are, according to NCLB, "highly qualified" has resulted in more and more requirements and restrictions for teacher preparation programs at the same time that alternative certification programs like ABCTE, Teach For America, and other fast-track programs are receiving more and more autonomy and flexibility. That is, at the same time that policymakers ask teacher preparation programs in higher education to do more to prepare teachers for certification, often with less funding, they authorize and fund fast-track programs that, by definition, do less to prepare teachers for certification. This contradictory process functions not to raise the quality of teachers, but to undermine teacher preparation in higher education, which will disproportionately impact high-needs schools (serving primarily communities of color and working-class communities), since such schools are the ones with the greatest shortage of certified teachers.

Significantly, it is no longer and perhaps never was the case that alternative certification is solely a Rightist issue. In Chicago, for example, alternative certification programs currently are receiving funding from a range of sources, including various foundations that seek immediate solutions to the teacher shortage problem in areas of high need. In Philadelphia, programs like Teach For America are partnering with teacher preparation programs that are led and staffed by faculty members whose research and teaching reflect or incorporate Leftist perspectives.

Similar contradictions and strange bedfellows can be seen in the regulation of schools. At the same time that regular public schools are becoming more centralized in their governance, more monitored in their performance on standardized tests, more restricted in their spending and hiring, and even more regulated in their curriculum and instruction (as with the increasing use of "teacher-proof," scripted curriculums), charter schools are receiving more autonomy and flexibility to meet the requirements of the state (Fuller, 2003). Charter schools are a type of public school for which a charter (or contract) has been created between educators/community members and the school district to operate in a particular way with the promise of particular results. The freedom of charter schools from many of the regulations placed on regular schools raises questions over whether such regulations were meant to improve public schools (since they are being made optional for the charter schools) or to encourage the creation of alteratives to public education. After all, some charter schools look more like private schools than public schools, with outsourced management, corporate funding, selective enrollments, and even religious bases. Seen in this way, the simultaneity of radical decentralization and privatization, alongside increased regulation of regular schools, suggests that, indeed, the larger purpose has been to undermine public education all along (Lipman, 2004).

Yet some people who support the availability of charter schools have other purposes in mind. Within communities of color, for example, some have turned away from a common school system that they believe has failed to serve their children and have conceptualized charter schools as an alternative space with the potential to affirm cultural differences and strengthen communities. Currently a higher proportion of Black and Latino/a students are in charter schools than regular public schools (Fuller, 2003). While charter schools may advance the privatization of public education, they also have the potential to address cultural differences as well as to localize accountability and make decision making more inclusive (Smith, 2001). Thus, for very different reasons, groups on both the Right and the Left believe that the public school system is failing to serve their needs and are turning to charter schools as a viable solution (Apple, 2001).

As with the supporters of alternative certification, the supporters of charter schools include groups from both the Right and the Left. It is not the case, then, that the Right or the Left is always defined by its support for or opposition to any particular issue. Being pro-charter does not necessarily make one Rightist, just as being anti-voucher does not make one Leftist. Both the Right and the Left can be on the same side of an issue, or can shift their position over time or in different contexts.

It is the rationale or the purpose behind the issue or initiative that differentiates the Right from the Left. But these underlying purposes often are not made explicit in public debates about education reform. What we hear are the messages that have been carefully crafted to influence our support for or opposition to an initiative. That is, masking the underlying purposes are carefully chosen frames.

CHAPTER 2

The Power of Frames

People do not necessarily vote in their self-interest. They vote their identities. They vote their values.

—George Lakoff, 2004, p. 19

"TRADITIONAL FAMILY" AND CORE VALUES

Examining the last few presidential elections, Lakoff (2004) notes how, at first glance, he had difficulty seeing what connected the vast range of issues that the Right—particularly Republicans—was fighting for (and, similarly, what connected the issues that the Left was fighting for). He did see, however, one theme that the Right kept revisiting, namely, "family values." This was perhaps not surprising, given the frequency with which the media as well as the general public conceptualized and talked about the nation through the metaphor of family, as with notions of the "founding fathers," "birth of a nation," "sending sons to war," and "daughters of the revolution." But he wondered why Republicans would keep talking about "family values" when so many other issues threatened national security and well-being, including nuclear proliferation and global warming. Perhaps it was not the issues that determined how people voted.

According to Lakoff, voters vote for what aligns with their identities and aspirational values, even if it means that they vote against their own self-interest, economic or otherwise. Successful candidates, therefore, are not those who run polls to determine the policy issues on which to run their campaigns, but rather those who succeed in tapping into something that lies deeper, at the voters' core sense of self, particularly their perception of who they are, who they would like to be, and what they value. In recent presidential elections, those core values reflected a particular image of the family.

There are two ways that most Americans, consciously or subconsciously, think about family. The "strict-father" family model is one in which the father is the leader of the family, knows right from wrong and teaches this to his children, disciplines his children when they go wrong, protects his family from the dangers outside, but does not dote on his children, which would serve as a crutch, and instead expects that they will "pull themselves up by their bootstraps" to make it. Intertwined with this family model are two other values: self-sufficiency, as captured by the rags-to-riches novels of 19th-century American author Horatio Alger in which young boys escape poverty through hard work; and meritocracy, where those who succeed are those with talent and perseverance. In contrast is the "nurturant-parent" family model in which parents are more equal in their relationship and in which children are nurtured in their growth rather than disciplined or left to fend for themselves. Many people understand and even identify with both family models, which is why the same person watching various television shows can feel a connection with strict-father families (as in "Father Knows Best") as well as with nurturant-parent families (as in "The Cosby Show").

What the Right has done is appropriate the strict-father model and frame its issues metaphorically around the components of this model. For example, like the strict father, the United States is seen as the leader of the world family, and like the father, we know what is right, we do not need to ask others like the United Nations for permission, and we punish, through embargoes or military campaigns, those who go wrong. We protect our families from the dangers "outside" the country with a strong military and with expensive military equipment, and from the dangers "outside" the community with more prisons and tougher sentencing. And just as fathers do not dote on their children, the government should not dote on its citizens through social welfare programs, environmental protection laws, education funding for disadvantaged communities, and so forth. What at first glance would seem disparate—militarization, incarceration, welfare, the environment, education—becomes connected to family values, resulting in the perception that, regardless of the issues, the Right or the Republican Party clearly shares "my" values. It should be noted that when those values are threatened, voters will be mobilized, as was arguably the case in recent elections and the role played by ballot initiatives and candidate platforms on same-sex marriage. Debates on same-sex marriage raise passion and controversy in U.S. society like few other topics, perhaps because same-sex marriage challenges the notion that the strict-father family is the only way that a family should be.

Historically, the strict-father family model has been used to regulate the teaching profession. At times, unmarried women were desirable as teachers because they did not cost much, so long as they left the profession when they got married and fulfilled their duties in the "traditional" family. At other times, unmarried women were undesirable as teachers because, if they were young, they were thought to dote too much on young boys, and if they were older, they were thought to dominate and, in the process, emasculate young boys (Blount, 1996).

Today the Right continues to use this strict-father model to frame education reform. The standards-and-testing movement that culminated in NCLB is illustrative. Leaders in education should know right from wrong and should prescribe what all students should learn (that is, there should be standards). Students, teachers, and schools should not be given assistance that can function as a crutch but, instead, should be treated equally and held accountable to reach the same standards and demonstrate that they have done so by way of standardized measures (there should be accountability). Schools, teachers, and students should be disciplined when they go wrong and fail to meet standards, as with cuts in funding to schools, loss of autonomy for principals, loss of placements for teachers, and denials of promotion or graduation for students (there should be sanctions). Parents should be able to protect their children from such dangers as lazy peers, unskilled teachers, or immoral school environments, and should have the choice of moving their children to other, better schools (there should be choice).

The four frames of standards, accountability, sanctions, and choice become linked together by a metaphor (the strict-father model) that makes the four frames inseparable from one another. The same is true for the frames of family, self-sufficiency, and meritocracy. These strategic framings, in which several frames link inseparably, help us to understand why Democrats who criticize, say, school choice but continue to use the language of accountability could be seen by some people to be contradictory or simply nonsensical.

The ability to frame the debate depends not only on the concept and the language used to convey that concept, but also on the means of communicating that language and on the frequency of the communication. In 2002, the Right spent four times as much as the Left on research and it got four times as much media time (Lakoff, 2004). Rightist leaders hold weekly meetings, led by strategist Grover Norquist, to work out their differences and develop their common messages. Rightist foundations invest heavily in those institutions and projects that can market their policy priorities (Krehely, House, & Kernan, 2004). The Right puts vast resources into ensuring that it is framing the debate.

Of course, the Right has not relied only on the frame of family values to advance its policy agendas. As noted above, the strict-father family model works hand-in-hand with particular notions of self-sufficiency and meritocracy—notions that are best captured by an ideology that currently drives the U.S. political economy and its control over the global distribution of capital, namely, neoliberalism.

"FREE ENTERPRISE" AND COMMON SENSE

This "neo" liberalism is usually presented not as a particular set of interests and political interventions, but as a kind of nonpolitics—a way of being reasonable, and of promoting universally desirable forms of economic expansion and democratic government around the globe. Who could be against greater wealth and more democracy?

—Lisa Duggan, 2003, p. 10

Neoliberalism can best be understood within the historical context of the Right's emergence. The 1970s was a time when various groups began coalescing to counter what they perceived as a Leftist attack on the American "free enterprise" system, and at the helm of this emerging Right were wealthy conservatives whose philanthropic work helped to seed what eventually grew into an interconnected web of organizations and initiatives. Their project was as much legislative as it was ideological, meaning that they aimed as much to impact legislation and policy as they did to shape "common sense" in society, particularly regarding those ideas that fuel the American "free enterprise" system and its resulting economic disparities. The emerging ideology was that of neoliberalism, which values competitive markets and the freedom of individual choice within them, and devalues governmental or cultural attempts to redistribute resources or accountability. Thus, it often manifests itself in policies that reduce governmental regulation of trade, increase the privatization of public services, and support the growth of businesses.

Although germinating in the 1940s and 1950s, this pro-business ideology and movement began to significantly frame economic policy beginning in the 1980s, as exemplified by the "Washington Consensus," which was a set of policy frames regarding fiscal austerity, privatization, market liberalization, and governmental stabilization that were created and implemented by the International Monetary Fund, U.S. Treasury, World Bank, and World Trade Organization. According to Lisa Duggan (2003), the pro-business strategy was threefold: to present neoliberal policies as politically neutral concepts of what makes for good management or effective operation (that is, as simply "good" business practice) while obscuring the underlying cultural values and benefits for those in power; to change alliances and policy issues while maintaining an underlying neoliberal agenda; and perhaps most important, to fuel the debates between Republicans and Democrats on what is "conservative" or "liberal" while ignoring or masking how both sides of the debate are already framed by neoliberalism. The success of the neoliberal movement can be understood in large part in terms of its ability to go unquestioned, to be taken for granted as the way things are and/or should be. And indeed, the "Washington Consensus" became so taken-for-granted that although the U.S. presidency and Congress have since shifted back and forth between being controlled by Republicans and Democrats, U.S. economic policy throughout has remained firmly within neoliberal ideology. Pro-business activists have succeeded in getting both political parties to take neoliberalism for granted and to support policies that, at their core, raise corporate profits and benefit the wealthy at the expense of labor and consumers, thus exacerbating economic disparities.

Two aspects of neoliberalism help to advance the pro-business agenda: privatization and personal responsibility (Duggan, 2003). Privatization is the restructuring of public services into a market-like industry that results in the shifting of funds, oversight, and accountability from government to individuals and/or corporations. With privatization, economic enterprises become treated as "private" matters, not under the domain of public, governmental regulation or intrusion, and profit (or loss) becomes a private matter as well, whereby those who choose to work hard and are able to work well should reap the rewards. This latter point is what connects privatization with the commonly expressed values of freedom and meritocracy, thus making it a policy initiative that many Americans will want to support. Hand-in-hand with the concept of privatization is that of personal responsibility, which is the reliance on oneself rather than on others, and consequently the rejection of political or social welfare structures that could hamper one's own sense of independence and develop instead a system of unfair distribution of resources and/or undeserved rewards. Drawing on liberal-humanist notions of individual agency and freedom, neoliberalism overlooks structural or institutional biases, historical legacies regarding oppression and injustice, and an economic structure with built-in mechanisms that exacerbate inequalities. Neoliberalism, in other words, promotes an understanding of equality and freedom that presumes a level playing field.

Several of the education policy initiatives from the Right presume a level playing field. NCLB imposes a system of standards and accountability that provides little accommodation for students who begin the academic year with talents and challenges that differ from the norm in their school. The "65% Solution" standardizes school district spending as if all districts have the same needs and comparable resources. Tax limitation measures disproportionately impact healthcare and education spending, harming the populations that access those public services the most. School voucher programs put public schools in competition with private schools for student enrollment, as if all schools have comparable resources to compete, and furthermore as if all parents were equally capable of and willing to participate (which is not the case because White and middle-class parents are much more likely to participate than others; see Apple, 2001). Neoliberalism and its presumption of a level playing field rely on decontextualized notions of equality and fairness that mask structural inequities. Indeed, this masking of structural problems is a function of other frames from the Right, particularly frames about the relationship of the United States to other nations and peoples.

"BEACON OF GOODNESS" AND DISTRACTION

On September the 11th, enemies of freedom committed an act of war against our country. . . . Americans are asking, why do they hate us? They hate what we see right here in this chamber—a democratically elected government. . . . They hate our freedoms. . . . This is not, however, just America's fight. . . . This is civilization's fight. This is the fight of all who believe in progress and pluralism, tolerance and freedom.

—President George W. Bush,
in a speech to Congress on September 20, 2001

I'm amazed that there's such misunderstanding of what our country is about that people would hate us. I am—like most Americans, I just can't believe it because I know how good we are.

—President George W. Bush,
in a press conference on October 11, 2001

In the spring of 2004, images of naked brown bodies in sexualized situations flashed on television and computer screens across the United States and the world. More and more photographs and personal testimonies had surfaced of abuse inflicted on Iraqi prisoners by members of the U.S. military. Some of the abuse involved a mockery or forced abdication of religion, as when prisoners were compelled to denounce their Islamic beliefs, give thanks to Jesus, consume prohibited foods and drinks, abstain from prayer and worship, undress in front of others, and simulate or engage in prohibited sex acts (Fay, 2004). This was perhaps not surprising: The tragedies of September 11, 2001 were largely understood to be those of a religious or holy war (a *jihad*) against the United States. Although not all in the Arab region are Muslim, and vice versa, and not all Arabs and Muslims subscribed to this anti-U.S. stance, many in the United States embraced the discourse perpetuated by political leaders and the media that conflated race, religion, and political ideology into the category of "Arab-Muslim terrorist" (Chon & Yamamoto, 2003).

This racialization of the Arab-Muslim, when put alongside a newly rationalized fear toward this group as "terrorist," resulted in abuse that targeted not only religious difference. Much of the abuse was also sexual in nature, which is, again, perhaps not surprising. Within the United States, racialized oppression has long operated alongside the oppression of sexuality and sex for men of color, as in post–Civil War lynching of Black men that involved physical castration (Pinar, 2001). Even stereotypes and representations of men of color have long involved some sexualization of the male body, as with Black American men stereotyped as oversexed and oversized, or Asian American men stereotyped as asexual and small (Kumashiro, 2002).

In Iraq, for the most part, it was male guards who forced male prisoners to undress for others to see for extended periods of time. Prisoners were placed in human pyramids or other positions in which their naked bodies were in contact, and some were forced to simulate or even engage in same-sex sexual activity with one another. Some guards themselves were perpetrators of forced sodomy with foreign objects and of various forms of rape. Such abuse should not be considered homoerotic by mere coincidence, and should not be dismissed as the acts of sadistic homosexuals. As has been known to happen in college fraternity initiations, straight-identified men often subject other straight-identified men to homoerotic situations as a gendered enactment of power, as a way to feminize another group, sometimes playfully but sometimes not (Sanday, 1990).

It was in these sexual aspects of the Iraqi prisoner abuse that we saw manifest on a physical, visceral level a new form of Orientalism (Said, 1979). Orientalism can be traced back 2,000 years, to a time when European explorers of Asia and the Middle East began crafting tales of a mystical "Orient," a place where the landscape, the food, even the bodies of the human inhabitants were fundamentally different than and inferior to their own. By subordinating Asia and the Middle East within an imagined patriarchal relationship between the feminized East and the masculinized West, Europeans convinced themselves that they had a moral responsibility to make the "Orient" more civilized. According to Said, this relationship took on physical and sexual symbolism as a male Europe was to arouse, penetrate, and possess the "Eastern bride." The impact of this relationship went beyond the symbolic as Europeans colonized different parts of the East and profited from the area's natural and human resources.

While the abuse of Iraqi prisoners could have been portrayed as the newest manifestation of Orientalism and of the history of gendered racism in the United States, such was not the case. Political leaders were quick to denounce the abuse and joined the public outrage against the individuals whose presumably singular sadism or irresponsibility made such abuse possible. People seemed surprised that Americans could inflict such abuse, even in a time of war. The abuse was not seen as indicative of the colonialist, racist, and sexist relations that the United States had long had with Asia and the Middle East. Rather, the abuse was seen as an anomaly, a distraction from what was otherwise a mutually beneficial relationship. In fact, the public discourse seemed to focus entirely on the graphic images of abuse, on the spectacle of soldiers-gone-bad, making it possible to ignore or even mask the less overt and more systemic forms of oppression. Ironically, the abuse was a physical manifestation of the Orientalist relationship of the United States with the East, but when sensationalized by the media, it functioned to distract attention from that very relationship.

This should not be surprising. U.S. imperialism, which aims to impose the U.S. social system onto others, operates precisely by making itself invisible to the general U.S. population (Johnson, 2000). Through law and policy, education, and popular culture, U.S. imperialism operates by framing the U.S. social system as superior, natural, and inevitable, and its "expansion" to other nations is taken as a sign of those nations' development and progress. Furthermore, when imperialist actions in the form of punitive economic policy and military action are unmasked or leaked, they are described as anomalies and not as indicators of ongoing U.S. policies of violence and subordination. People in the United States do not often see U.S. imperialism, instead wondering, "What American empire?" (Isaac, 2006).

It is important to ask, then, what it would mean for the public to learn to read about manifestations of oppression in alternative ways, in ways that raise awareness of and challenge the oppressions from which imperialist actions originated. Alternative ways of framing oppression and its manifestations do exist. One example can be found in fiction. The image of a White U.S. soldier raping a brown-bodied prisoner in the East reminded me of a short story titled "The Shoyu Kid" (Kaneko, 1976) about a group of young boys in a Japanese American internment camp during World War II. In this story, the manifestation of Orientalism is the molestation of a Japanese American boy by a White U.S. soldier. As with the Iraqi abuse, the molesting of a Japanese American boy embodies the gendered language of West–East relations that is symbolic of Orientalism. But unlike the press coverage of the Iraqi abuse, the short story does not create a spectacle of the boy's molestation. In fact, the reader does not learn about the molestation except through implication since the only boy who observed the molestation refuses to describe what he saw. By not capturing the molestation in language or graphic detail, the story prevents readers from feeling that they fully understand what happened, and in doing so, prevents the readers from feeling outraged at only the individuals in that one act. The silence around the act of molestation keeps that act from becoming known as only a singular occurrence, thus helping to drive the story around a broader understanding of what that act represents, namely, the oppression of Japanese Americans.

Therein lies the pedagogical potential of the framing of this oppressive act. The boys who learn of the molestation do not direct their frustration at the individual soldier alone. To them, the soldier and the molested boy symbolize how "everyone" is "queer." As the boys commiserate in silence, one of them throws rocks at but misses the sign with the camp's name on it, thereby physically acting out and demonstrating their frustration at things beyond their control (Eng, 2001). There the story ends, inviting the reader to ask critical questions about the meaning of the molestation in the context of the Japanese American internment. The story does not frame the molestation as a spectacle or anomaly. Rather, it frames the molestation as something that we could not bear to know, and in our struggle to know, we are compelled to interrupt our complicity with what it represents.

Admittedly, there are formidable challenges to learning to read in ways that ask critical questions about the broader context of individual acts. Today, perhaps one of the greatest challenges to such critical questioning can be seen in the climate of fear that has been cultivated in the United States post–9/11—a fear that compels us to comply.

"BE VERY AFRAID"

The people can always be brought to the bidding of the leaders. This is easy. All you have to do is tell them they are being attacked and denounce the peacemakers for lack of patriotism and exposing the country to danger. It works the same in any country.

—Nazi Reich Marshall Hermann Goering, Nuremberg War Trials

I was sitting in my office on the morning of September 11, 2001, when a colleague rushed to my door to tell me that she had just heard that an airplane had crashed into one of the World Trade Center towers in New York City. As the hours passed, more airplanes crashed, both of the towers collapsed, a part of the Pentagon in Washington, DC, was destroyed, and all attention seemed to turn to the terror that had hit U.S. soil. Thousands were presumed to have died, forthcoming tragedies were not ruled out, and the nation seemed paralyzed with grief, fear, and uncertainty. Classes were cancelled at the college where I was teaching, so I headed home, glued to the radio, and then the television. I wept as I saw many die and heard many witnesses tell their stories of panic and loss. Some of the attackers passed through the airport not far from where I was then living in Maine. I had friends and relatives living in New York City and Washington, DC. I hoped that they were safe. And I hoped that I was safe.

Many people wanted answers. These were not tragic coincidences. These were planned attacks. Why would people want to attack "us"? How could people be so "evil"? Who is responsible? How will we punish "them"? Mixed in with grief, fear, and uncertainty was a profound sense of anger. I remember not being able to eat very much that day. My nausea was but one of the indications that I was, indeed, overcome with sadness and fear. But unlike many others, my feelings of sadness and fear resulted not only from acknowledging the attacks on U.S. soil and the deaths left in their wake, but also from anticipating how many in the United States would respond. News commentators were speculating that this was an act of terrorism by Muslim extremists, and political leaders were promising to use all at their disposal to punish those responsible for this "worst act of terrorism on U.S. soil." People wanted revenge. And I feared that in the name of revenge, many would be unwilling or even unable to recognize the oppressiveness of their own responses. I suspected that many would respond in terribly oppressive ways. My fears were justified.

As U.S. intelligence agencies gathered evidence that "Muslim extremists" were responsible for these attacks, the responses were swift and violent. Abroad, the United States sent more and more military forces to find and punish "those responsible." Political leaders called for a war on terrorism that would span not only the Middle East but also the entire globe in an effort to eliminate those who sought to "attack freedom and democracy." Within the United States, more and more individuals seemed to think this war was against anyone who "looked Muslim" or "looked Arab," including those who wore a turban or headwrap or simply had darker skin. Such Muslim- or Arab-looking people were treated as potential criminals. They were carefully, even aggressively, scrutinized when trying to board airplanes, and were subject to harassment and abuse. In the months that followed September 11th, the number of reports of hate-related incidences and hate crimes against individuals who looked Muslim or Arab increased dramatically in the United States (Coen, 2001).

Although political leaders were quick to denounce such racial and religious scapegoating, they themselves were guilty of similar acts of harassment and discrimination. As agencies responsible for fighting terrorism began arresting or harassing many they suspected of being connected to the attacks, or to future attacks, and denying many of them their constitutional rights, political leaders were granting more and more powers of surveillance to these agencies to fight terrorism, particularly through the 2001 PATRIOT Act (American Civil Liberties Union, 2001). In fact, in an eerie parallel to the Japanese American internment during World War II, hundreds upon hundreds of people, including Muslim Americans and Americans of Middle Eastern descent, were rounded up and interned. More and more initiatives were launched to expand the ability of the government to gather information on how we spend our money, what we read in the library or on the Internet, where we travel and when, what we do in our spare time and with whom—and this information could come via our neighbors and private companies in ways of which we were not even aware. These increased powers may have conflicted with our constitutional and civil rights, but polls indicated that the majority in the United States supported such a compromise (Taylor, 2001).

This was, after all, a time for the nation to come together. We should stand behind our political leaders and present ourselves as a strong, united nation. We should be proud to be part of the United States and display this pride with flags on our shirts and our cars and our desks and our lawns. After all, the United States was said to symbolize freedom and democracy, and to attack the United States was to attack these institutions as well. The pressure to conform to these convictions was significant, as was the penalty for failing to do so. Representative Barbara Lee of California, the sole Congressperson who voiced dissent for the president's war policies, received death threats (Carlson, 2001). Even in my own neighborhood, news that individuals were being attacked verbally and physically for being "anti-American" prompted a woman and her family to take down a sign from their apartment window that read, "Give peace a chance." Being "American" required acting in only certain ways and wanting only certain things.

People were afraid and were kept in a state of fear as the government constantly raised and lowered and raised again the official "terror alert." The media constantly reminded us that the "terrorists" were still out there, planning their next attacks, and although U.S. intelligence was successful in thwarting one attack after another, the "terrorists" continued to evade capture. So long as the enemy was out there, the American public would continue to turn to what it perceived to be a source of strength: strength in our sense of national identity and unity, strength in our president and his ability to fight back.

We are now learning that the president might have been lying about the reasons to go to war, and with whom, and where and when (Moore, 2004). It might have been the case that the United States was not as much the "innocent victim" as the media would have us believe. What some people call terrorist attacks on freedom and democracy can be understood as "blowback." First used internally at the U.S. Central Intelligence Agency, the term "blowback" refers to the unintended consequences of policies and actions abroad that were kept secret from the American public (Johnson, 2000). Many acts of "terrorism" can be understood as blowback from U.S. policies and actions over the past half-century. But this is not often explained, and purposefully so. After all, it might be that the fear we feel is generated in part by those businesses that profit most when we support paying more for greater security, including to contractors and businesses with ties to the Bush Administration (Moore, 2004). Much can be accomplished when people are afraid. From the financial benefits of business contracts, to the social benefits for the wealthy of a reduced welfare state, to the political benefits for the Bush Administration of increased unity and conformity, there is great profit in the business of fear.

Within education, fear similarly drives reform. For over 2 decades the public has been told to fear that the United States is a "nation at risk" of problems. Domestically, a large percentage of students are failing, especially in poorer communities with fewer resources and presumably—or, some would argue, "consequently"—more crime. Abroad, students from some countries are outperforming U.S. students on standardized tests. Critics argue that students in U.S. schools are failing to learn what is needed to succeed in the workplace and the global market, forcing the nation to devote more of its resources to addressing social ills while compromising its position as a world leader in military strength, scientific achievement, democratic values, and political influence.

If the United States is faltering, and if people believe that things were better in the past, as they "traditionally" were, then people are likely to want things to be as they were back then. And if education "back then" was better and is faltering now because of the various "trends" in education reform like student-centered classrooms, experiential learning, multicultural curriculums, and differentiated instruction and assessment, then people are likely to revert to commonsense notions of how schools were and should be. People will want to see schools teaching primarily the academic subjects, like the "three Rs" of reading, writing, and arithmetic; or standardized curriculums being used that level the playing field by teaching everyone the same thing; or students scoring well on tests as evidence that they have learned; or teachers using instructional methods that "work" (as categorized by the U.S. Department of Education's "What Works" Clearinghouse). Indeed, NCLB illustrates such ideas by making explicit what and how teachers are supposed to teach—going back to the "basics," aligning all lessons to learning standards, using high-stakes tests to determine student promotion and graduation, and sticking to scripted curriculums and other instructional methods that are "scientifically proven" to be effective (U.S. Department of Education, 2002).

The fear over a failing education system has helped to advance the standards-and-testing movement, which in turn creates opportunities for profit. Scripted curriculums require textbooks, worksheets, teacher guides, and other materials to be purchased by schools or districts. High-stakes tests require testing sheets, scoring services, tutoring services, study guides, and other materials, also to be purchased by schools or states. Defining only certain methods to be "scientifically proven" privileges certain kinds of research in competition for funding, publishing, and other forms of support. Even the delineation of learning standards is profitable, perhaps not financially, but socially and politically. Throughout the 20th century, schools have been critiqued for teaching in ways that reinforce a particular racial, class, gender, and national consciousness that privileges certain groups and marginalizes others, helping us to understand why the debate over what to include in the standards is a political and highly contested one (Pinar, Reynolds, Slattery, & Taubman, 2000). By regulating what to teach, the learning standards can privilege certain knowledge, skills, and perspectives, particularly the knowledge, skills, and perspectives of those groups that are defining the standards (Apple, 2001).

What is important here is the recognition that the frame of fear intersects with and reinforces the other frames, as illustrated in Figure 2.1. Fear is what prompts us to look to "traditional" values for a sense of who we are and where we went awry. Fear is what pushes us to place faith in a "free enterprise" system that purportedly brings out the best in each of us through competition. Fear is

FIGURE 2.1. Translating Priorities into Frames

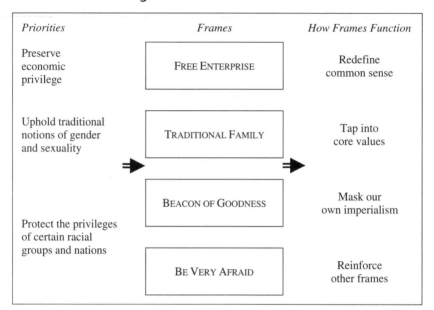

what calls on us to unite behind and comply with our leaders as we search for strength in the face of adversity. The frame of fear, in other words, helps to cohere the various priorities of the Right and makes its initiatives inseparable.

CHAPTER 3

Appropriation of Frames About "Safety"

Within the last decade . . . some on the Christian right realized
that excessively vitriolic condemnation of homosexuals was not
the best political strategy. . . . By embracing the ex-gay movement
and reframing their attack on homosexuality in gentler terms, the
Christian right acquired the cover to promote a reactionary agenda
that attempts to deny LGBT people any legal rights and protections.
. . . Furthermore, the "love the sinner, hate the sin" rhetoric enables
the Christian right to be more appealing to moderate voters who do
not consider themselves to be homophobic but feel uncomfortable
about the "gay lifestyle."

—Jason Cianciotto & Sean Cahill, 2006, p. 25

THE TROUBLE WITH SAFETY

Research has long documented various forms of bias against lesbian, gay, bisexual, transgender, and self-identified "queer" (LGBTQ) people in schools, from disturbingly high rates of bullying and harassment, to indifference and homophobia among school personnel, to invisibility and misinformation about LGBTQ people in the curriculum, to heterosexist assumptions made about students and their families (Epstein, O'Flynn, & Telford, 2001). Across the United States, a range of initiatives is underway to address these biases, primarily around the problem of bullying and harassment. Indeed, the goal of making schools safer for LGBTQ students has become the focal point of initiatives on policy, research, funding, training, and student organizing, at least among the most visible organizations of the Left. The Gay, Lesbian, and Straight Education Network (GLSEN), for example, has researched the links between policy and safety, and has documented the decreased rate of bullying and harassment and the increased likelihood of adult intervention when school district policies explicitly include sexual orientation and gender identification within the list of categories protected from discrimination and harassment (Kosciw & Diaz, 2006). Consequently, because most states do not have such inclusive policies, changing nondiscrimination policies to include sexual orientation and gender identification among the protected categories has become a central goal of GLSEN's state-based lobbying efforts.

A few years ago, I was a participant at a national roundtable for researchers and advocates that was convened by the National Gay and Lesbian Task Force and that produced a report on the state of education and educational policy for LGBTQ students (Cianciotto & Cahill, 2003). At the roundtable, we debated whether to continue highlighting the problems of bullying and harassment that LGBTQ students confront in schools or to focus on, say, issues of resilience, agency, and self-advocacy among the youth. Because we generally agreed that funders are more likely to be moved by the problems than by the strengths of youth, the discussion and the subsequent report remained focused on the problem of safety.

Similarly, the National Education Association focused on the problem of school safety when creating its new National Training Program on Safety, Bias, and GLBT Issues. At the time, I was on staff at NEA and was responsible for creating and coordinating this program. NEA's internal research revealed that the language of safety is what brings many educators—including its own members, who identified with the Right on some issues—on board with the goal of addressing anti-LGBTQ bias, and the training program and associated materials that I created needed to align with this message. Youth organizations, like the Gay–Straight Alliance (GSA) Network, have countered misrepresentations of GSAs as "sex clubs" by emphasizing their goal of bringing gay and straight allied youth together in order to "create safe environments, educate the school community about homophobia, and fight discrimination, harassment, and violence in schools" (http://www.gsanetwork.org).

Of course, safety is a fundamental human right of all students, and because there is a profound lack of safety for LGBTQ students in and out of school, our nation must do much more to make schools safer for all. I have led one and been centrally involved in another effort in this regard, and I will continue to be involved in such efforts in the future. However, it is important to recognize that this primary focus on safety does have significant drawbacks. There are at least three.

First, the issue of safety focuses attention on homophobia and bias against gender nonconformity, on the *marginalizing* of LGBTQS, and not on heterosexism and the *privileging* of heterosexuality, and therefore focuses on the manifestation of the problem rather than its root cause. Advocates point to the need to reduce homophobia in schools, such as the name-calling, bullying, gay-bashing, and ostracism that target LGBTQ students; they focus, in other words, on how we think about and treat homosexuality and gender nonconformity. Left unexamined are the ways that we think about and treat heterosexuality and gender norms, including the prevailing assumptions that heterosexuality and gender conformity are the natural, normal, better, or moral way to be. And therein lies the problem. The field of queer studies has long argued that LGBTQ identities are devalued and marginalized only because heterosexual and gender-conforming identities are, in contrast, valued and privileged (Butler, 1993; Pinar, 1998).

There cannot be a "normal" sexual orientation if there is not simultaneously an abnormal or queer sexual orientation, and there would not be advantages to being "normal" if there were not disadvantages to being queer. Privileging heterosexuality *requires* the marginalizing of homosexuality, which is why attempts to reduce homophobia cannot succeed without also addressing heterosexism (Britzman, 1998). The problem, of course, is that heterosexism is a much harder thing to "see," which helps to explain why even among those who advocate for safety, there is doubt that such a thing as heterosexism exists. Agreement may exist that harassment is a problem and should be stopped, but disagreement persists over whether any other lesson or even conversation on different sexualities and genders belongs in school, including discussions to raise awareness of sexual diversity, students' identities, and, especially, the privileging of heterosexuality and gender conformity. By not challenging this hetero-normativity and gender-normativity (the notion that everyone should be heterosexual and gender conforming), those initiatives that define the problem fundamentally as one of safety define the goal as simply a school where such harassment does not occur or is not apparent.

This leads to the second drawback, namely that the focus on safety can be interpreted as advancing assimilation, especially when the scope of "addressing anti-LGBTQ bias" is limited to the reduction of harassment. Defining the problem solely in terms of harassment not only overlooks the many other ways that bias plays out, but also implies that the problem ultimately arises from the LGBTQ students themselves, the thinking being that, "There would be no anti-LGBTQ bullying if students were not LGBTQ, or at least were not LGBTQ in uncomfortable ways." If this were the case, the solution would be quite problematic: LGBTQ students should simply be more like straight students, look as they look, and interact as they interact. Indeed, a common response to the argument that LGBTQ students are harassed at disturbingly high rates is to blame the victim, to say that they would not be so harassed if they were not so "obviously gay," and further to point to the counterexample of gender-conforming or "properly" gendered LGBTQ students who refute claims of bias and danger because they do not "draw attention" to their sexual or gender differences. Safety would not be a problem if LGBTQ students only learned to assimilate their difference.

Blaming the victim ties in with my third point: The language of safety has become appropriated by the Right. Extremists may continue to argue that LGBTQ people deserve abuse and even death, but some on the Right have spoken out and insisted that the bullying and harassment so frequently experienced by LGBTQ youth should be stopped. Significantly, the reasons they give are not merely because bullying is morally wrong. Mixed with the implication

that "you wouldn't get bullied if you weren't gay," is the implication that "you wouldn't feel hurt by the bullying if you weren't
weakened by being gay," or on the flipside, "if you had the strength
to end the bullying that targets you, you'd also have the strength
to stop being gay." A recently released resource booklet for youth
leaders interested in helping to change gay youth into straight ones
implies such messages when it states the following:

> Men and women who struggle with [same-sex attraction] often
> come from backgrounds of abuse and isolation from family, peers or
> both. . . . Many strugglers wrongly assume that this abuse occurred
> because of their supposedly inborn homosexuality, when in real-
> ity this abuse exacerbates feelings of inadequacy and is a primary
> source of the same-sex attracted person's struggle. Homosexuality
> (like a lot of sinful addictions) is an issue of *broken relationships* and
> *distorted identity.* Verbal and physical abuse *strengthen* the *lies* that
> keep people in *bondage* to *sin.*" (Exodus Youth, n.d., p. 41, emphasis
> in original)

So, yes, bullying should be stopped, but not merely to protect
LGBTQ youth; rather, it should be stopped so that they can more
likely be changed.

These limitations of the Left's primary focus on school safety
raise questions about whether the Left's work of addressing anti-
LGBTQ bias is best framed, at this point in time, primarily by the
issue of safety.

THE INSTITUTIONALIZATION OF BIAS

The Right does not focus primarily on safety. Recent controversies
reveal Rightist initiatives that institutionalize anti-LGBTQ bias in a
variety of ways. The activism of Chicago educator-scholar-activists
Erica Meiners and Therese Quinn has helped to generate awareness of and controversy over three current initiatives (http://www.
therese-othereye.blogspot.com). The first is an initiative by the
national accrediting agency for institutions that prepare teachers

for initial state certification to teach in public schools, namely the National Council for Accreditation of Teacher Education (NCATE). In the past decade, NCATE increasingly has come to shape teacher education programs by delineating those standards against which the programs are evaluated and, by implication, with which they must align their curriculum, practices, and program structures. Although many institutions do not pursue NCATE accreditation and are accredited only through their state's department of education, more and more institutions do pursue NCATE accreditation, and an increasing number of states model their accrediting process on NCATE, thus leaving institutions in those states with no choice but to pursue NCATE-based accreditation.

Not surprisingly, in a profession as diverse as teacher education across the United States, NCATE's standards that address diversity and bias have been contested. As NCATE undertook a revision of its standards in early 2006, it deleted the term "social justice" from its glossary and main text. Early that fall, hundreds of teacher educators learned of this proposed revision and protested to NCATE with an open letter (available at http://www.therese-othereye. blogspot.com). Included in that letter was the related concern that two dimensions of diversity have never been included in the main text of the standards where "diversity" is explained, namely sexual orientation and gender identification, even though these two dimensions are connected to disturbingly high rates of bullying and harassment in schools. Without inclusion of social justice and sexual orientation/gender identification, outsiders such as accreditation review teams and insiders such as faculty members within the programs have less foundation on which to push programs that are not yet addressing, or not adequately addressing, these issues.

In its defense, NCATE (2006) explained that it "does not expect or require institutions to inculcate candidates with any particular social or political ideology." It categorized "social justice," including the curtailing of anti-LGBTQ bias, as something outside the realm of professional responsibility, as an "ideology," and thus as something that conflicts with NCATE's and, by extension, the teacher education profession's, presumption of political neutrality. The problem here is that NCATE's silence on social justice and sexual orientation/ gender identification is not a neutral stance, but one that makes a political statement. Its silence implies that teacher education programs are not required to be responsible for preparing teachers to address the injustices that already exist, including anti-LGBTQ bias. Its silence allows anti-LGBTQ bias to continue unchallenged.

The second initiative occurred at the state level and involved the Illinois Association for Colleges of Teacher Education (IACTE) and the Illinois Board of Higher Education (IBHE). IACTE varies the location of its semiannual conference, and in the fall of 2006 held its conference on the campus of Wheaton College. Wheaton, a Christian college, asks all members of its college community to join and abide by what it calls its Community Covenant (available at http:// www.wheaton.edu), which establishes a set of standards and regulations that students have come to call "the pledge." Applicants for admission to the College must sign a statement confirming that they have read and agree to the Covenant. Among the requirements of the Covenant is to abide by the Scripture which, according to the pledge, condemns "sexual immorality, such as the use of pornography, pre-marital sex, adultery, homosexual behavior and all other sexual relations outside the bounds of marriage between a man and woman." Wheaton is not alone among Christian colleges in its explicit condemnation. According to Soulforce (http://www. soulforce.org), which is an advocacy organization that works for the freedom of LGBTQ people from religious and political oppression, over 200 colleges in the United States have policies that ban the enrollment of LGBTQ students or that otherwise explicitly discriminate against LGBTQ students.

A group of teacher educators protested the meeting location, pointing out that even though attendees of the conference were not required to take the pledge in order to enter the campus, the decision to hold a public meeting in a place that explicitly states its condemnation of same-sex sexual behavior and, by extension, of the people who are in same-sex relationships shows disregard for LGBTQ people who attended or wanted to attend the conference, and also highlights the state's indifference to institutionalized bias. Indeed, the state agency that oversees accreditation, IBHE, has accredited Wheaton College for teacher certification, which means that the state has chosen to approve the program run by a college that explicitly states its anti-LGBTQ bias. In doing so, IBHE has sanctioned anti-LGBTQ bias not only in Wheaton College, but in Illinois public schools as well, since Wheaton graduates, all of whom signed their agreement with the Covenant, can be certified to teach in public schools. Wheaton graduates can expect to have LGBTQ students on their campuses and in their classrooms, just as Illinois LGBTQ students can expect that some of their teachers may have pledged to abide by homophobic standards with the blessing of the state. Such teachers will not likely be prepared to adequately address the anti-LGBTQ bias that permeates schools, and may even actively contribute to that bias.

Anti-LGBTQ bias officially exists in a number of public institutions, not only education. Perhaps most notable is the U.S. military, which battled President Clinton in 1992 over whether to continue barring gay and lesbian people from serving in the military and reached the now-infamous compromise: Don't ask (if someone is gay), Don't tell (if you are). This leads to the third initiative, which occurred in 2006 in the Chicago Public School (CPS) District. Currently, CPS is undergoing a reform initiative called "Renaissance 2010," which is a restructuring program that aims to open 100 new schools by 2010 to replace failing schools (http://www.ren2010.cps.k12.il.us/overren.shtml). In the fall of 2006, Senn High School was restructured, dividing its building space to make room for a new naval academy that incorporates militarism into its curriculum and culture. Community organizations protested the installation of the naval academy for several reasons: The process of deciding to create a naval academy did not involve community residents; military-themed schools have not demonstrated that they are able to raise student learning; and the incorporation of military themes into the curriculum and culture of the school conflicted with the values of some community residents who disagreed with U.S. foreign policies of militarization, as well as U.S. domestic policies of targeting young men of color in poorer communities for military recruitment (Save Senn Coalition, n.d.).

Furthermore, this new naval academy would be modeled on the military, which has institutionalized bias against gays and lesbians, as well as a culture that historically has overlooked sexism against women and reinforced rigid gender norms. As with IBHE's accreditation of Wheaton College, the district's incorporation of the U.S. military into its schools gives the schools reason to ignore bias based on gender and sexual orientation, and even to reinforce this bias by teaching that LGBTQ people do not belong in the school, as they do not belong in the military. In fact, the extension of anti-LGBTQ discrimination is more than a hypothesis since the JROTC prohibits employment of gays and lesbians. Given the rise of harassment and discharge of LGBTQ personnel in the years following the "don't ask, don't tell" policy compromise, students have good reason to expect that the anti-LGBTQ climate already permeating schools may well worsen when put under a military theme.

THE CHRISTIAN RIGHT AND YOUTH

These moves to institutionalize anti-LGBTQ bias in education are not surprising given the ideological changes within the Right over the past few years, particularly the Christian Right, which currently leads the Right on such hot-button issues as homosexuality, abortion, and public education. In recent years, the Christian Right has become increasingly influenced by Christian Reconstructionism, which centers on the belief that Christ will not return until his kingdom is established on Earth (Lugg, 2000, 2001). Changes must be made here and now, not only in government, but also in public education, which is the institution that the Right often believes is hostile toward Christianity, particularly fundamentalist Christianity. So whereas Christian fundamentalists historically have stayed away from political involvement, the Christian Right has come to make control of government as well as education a top priority.

The Christian Right is involved in a range of education policy issues, some that are explicitly about Christianity and some that are not. Examples include allowing for prayer in schools and Bible Clubs; formally teaching the Bible and such biblical contents as creationism, also known as "intelligent design"; prohibiting schools from doing what the Christian Right finds objectionable, which can range from teaching evolution (or teaching evolution without also teaching "intelligent design") to using books with content that it finds controversial; and allowing students to form gay–straight alliances or in any way to be taught that being gay is acceptable.

Recently, the Christian Right has changed the terms of its involvement in "gay issues." Beginning in the early 1970s, following the landmark decision by the American Psychiatric Association to remove homosexuality from its list of disorders, the Christian Right offered to save homosexuals from going to hell by changing their sexual orientation through "transformational" ministries and "reparative" therapies. Its targets were primarily lesbian, gay, and bisexual adults. But starting in the early 2000s, the Christian Right turned its attention to youth as it sought not merely to "cure" their homosexuality, but also to "prevent" them from becoming homosexual in the first place, including very young children with "pre-homosexual" tendencies that can manifest as gender nonconformity, as when boys act stereotypically feminine (Cianciotto & Cahill, 2006). One group engaged in sexual transformation is Focus on the Family, the largest evangelical Christian organization in the United States, which holds "Love Won Out" conferences for parents and youth (http://www.lovewonout.com). Another such group is Exodus International, an "ex-gay" organization for people who once identified as gay but no longer do, which has created a youth-programming arm called Exodus Youth that puts on "Groundswell" conferences for youth and people who work with them (http://groundswell2006.org). Both conferences focus on how to help homosexual youth or those "at risk" of becoming homosexual to not be so. In addition, a number of websites exist for youth, as well as online publications, blogs, and even comic books (see, for example, the resources and links on http://exodusyouth.net).

While gay marriage continues to stir heated emotions, one emerging and profoundly troubling battleground for "gay issues" is the education of young children. This was exemplified in January

2005 when two popular cartoon characters from children's television programs made the national news. One was SpongeBob SquarePants, an animated sponge who lives in a pineapple in an underwater city and who stars in one of the most watched programs on Nickelodeon. James Dobson, founder of Focus on the Family, along with the conservative Christian group American Family Association, raised awareness of an educational video, *We Are Family*, that was scheduled to be distributed to elementary schools across the country in March of that year (Kirkpatrick, 2005). The video featured over 100 characters from children's programs on three major networks (PBS, Nickelodeon, and Disney) singing the disco hit, "We Are Family," which some people consider to be a gay anthem. The Southern Poverty Law Center created lesson plans on tolerance to accompany the music video, and in their materials included sexual orientation as one of many dimensions of diversity. SpongeBob previously had been called "gay" because he holds hands with his sidekick, Patrick. For these reasons, according to Dobson, the video was "pro-homosexual," and although it was distributed on schedule, controversy ensued over whether the media had become too liberal and "pro-homosexual."

At around the same time, then newly appointed U.S. Secretary of Education Margaret Spellings raised controversy over Buster. In a PBS children's show, *Postcards from Buster*, the animated bunny Buster travels around the United States with his father to visit live, nonanimated people who show him and tell him about their area. In one episode, Buster travels to Vermont and at one of the homes he visits he briefly meets the children (who are siblings) and their two mothers before learning about maple syrup and cheese. Spellings threatened to cut funding to PBS, arguing that "many parents would not want their young children exposed to the life-styles portrayed in this episode." According to a Department of Education spokesperson, "The episode is inappropriate for preschoolers ... one would be hard-pressed to explain how this serves as educational material for preschoolers" (de Moraes, 2005, p. C1). The episode was not aired nationally, although several local stations eventually did choose to air it. As with SpongeBob, the controversy over Buster raised public concern over whether young children were "too young" to learn about homosexuals.

Arguably, public perception of LGBTQ people has changed over the past few decades. From the Left, grassroots activism, AIDS activism, media representation, legislation and litigation, and "queer studies" have all contributed to more visibility, awareness, protection, and even acceptance of LGBTQ people and issues. Yet in the face of this progress some problems persist, like the epidemic levels of bullying of LGBTQ youth, and some problems are growing, like the state referenda prohibiting same-sex marriage or protection from anti-LGBTQ discrimination, and the nationwide organizing of outreach efforts to "cure" LGBTQ youth. As the Left has made gains in changing public perceptions about LGBTQ people, the Right has had to reframe the debate so as to continue receiving public support for initiatives that marginalize LGBTQ people.

APPROPRIATIONS OF FOUR FRAMES

The Right has developed four central frames for talking about LGBTQ issues in education. These frames mask the Right's underlying purposes primarily by appropriating frames that are commonly used by the Left.

Innocence

First, the frame of innocence. When Leftist advocates make the argument that schools need to do more to teach about LGBTQ people and issues, some people misinterpret this argument to be saying that schools should be teaching young children about "gay sex." Advocates have clarified their position by emphasizing three things: When talking about LGBTQ people, we are talking about famous people who happen to be LGBTQ; when talking about LGBTQ issues, we are talking about safety and bias; and given the wide range of ages in schools, we should and can talk about LGBTQ people and issues in age-appropriate ways. This was the framing 10 years ago with the documentary film *It's Elementary: Talking About Gay Issues in School* (Cohen & Chasnoff, 1996), which profiled several elementary and middle school teachers and their students as they engaged in lessons and discussions about gays and lesbians, diverse families, stereotypes, and biases. Similarly, this was the framing in 2006 with the legislative struggle in California regarding the Bias-Free Curriculum Act (SB 1437, vetoed in the fall of 2006). This act would have prohibited negative portrayals of LGBTQ people in the curriculum and, more controversially, would have called for the curricular inclusion of the contributions of LGBTQ people in California, but in ways appropriate to the subject being studied and the grade level of the students.

Ironically, the language of "age-appropriate" has opened the space for a shift in framing from the Right. "Age-appropriate" has both a descriptive and prescriptive element: It implies that younger children may not be ready to learn what older children can learn, but also implies that younger children should not be exposed to certain things. While often used in educational contexts to refer to cognitive appropriateness and how appropriate a lesson is to the child's current level of cognitive development, the term can easily be extended to questions of moral appropriateness and how moral it is to expose the child to an issue. According to the Right, exposing young children to LGBTQ issues puts them at risk of harm, or as the ex-gay movement suggests, puts them at risk of becoming LGBTQ, especially younger children who are weaker or simply more innocent to the ways of the world. Language around "age-appropriate," in other words, sometimes is used to justify the preservation of children's innocence from homosexuality for as long as possible, which makes the frame of children-as-innocent an extension and masking of the frame of homosexuality-as-contagion.

Of course, the notion that children should be kept away from homosexuality overlooks the reality that children learn quite a lot about homosexuality at very young ages from a range of sources, and that this learning often is filled with myths, stereotypes, and preconceptions about LGBTQ people. This is the insight in the opening scene of *It's Elementary*, in which elementary school students are asked to describe everything that comes to mind when they hear the words "gay" or "lesbian." They produce a list filled with stereotypes and misinformation, and then go on to explain that they have learned this (mis)information from a range of sources, including their families, their peers, and primarily the media. Children come to school having directly and indirectly learned a lot about LGBTQ people. Children are not innocent in the ways that this frame would have us believe, nor would we necessarily want them to be. After all, "innocent" often is used as a proxy for privileged social categories: children who are "still heterosexual," children who come from a "traditional family," or children who simply have not yet learned that there are ways of being other than heterosexual and gender-conforming. "Innocence" is a problematic concept (Rofes, 2005).

Neutrality

Similarly, schools themselves are never innocent or void of LGBTQ issues, which leads to the second frame, the frame of neutrality. Even without intending to, schools are places where LGBTQ issues—particularly anti-LGBTQ biases—arise constantly. For this reason, advocates of LGBTQ youth have argued that schools need to be places that are free of these forms of bias. I personally have worked with organizations to design and distribute posters that assert this goal of creating classrooms and schools that are "safe zones,"—spaces where all students, including LGBTQ students, are safe from bias.

The problem here is that bias can be defined in two ways: bias against LGBTQ people and bias in support of LGBTQ people. The Right similarly has argued that schools should be free of bias, where "bias" takes the form of any positive portrayal of LGBTQ people and issues. For the Right, teaching that it is okay to be gay is a form of political indoctrination from the Left. As with NCATE's understanding of "social justice," the Right, as in its opposition to California's Bias-Free Curriculum Act, has argued that schools should not inculcate such moral values or political ideology, and should instead focus on matters of academics—what often has been called the "three Rs" of reading, writing, and arithmetic—and leave any teaching of LGBTQ issues to institutions outside of the school, like the home or church. On LGBTQ issues, schools should be neutral or, more accurately, should appear to be neutral by being silent.

This distinction between being neutral and being silent is critical because schools can never be entirely neutral on "political" issues. Silence is not the same as neutrality. Silence can be biased, as when the failure to act in the face of discrimination serves to sanction such discrimination. Gaps in the curriculum also can be biased, as when the absence of groups of people or topics from the curriculum indirectly teaches that they are less important, or that the biases we already have formed against those groups or topics are valid and do not require correction. Decisions regarding curriculum, instruction, assessment, programming, culture, staffing, and so on are constantly being made that directly or indirectly bolster or challenge anti-LGBTQ bias: What gets included, and what, by default, gets excluded? Who speaks, and who does not? When and how is a topic emphasized, and when and how is it silenced? Because schools already are permeated with examples of anti-LGBTQ bias, they are already non-neutral, already biased against LGBTQ people, which means that when the Right advocates for schools to be "neutral" through silence, it is actually advocating for schools to continue normalizing or reinforcing the existing anti-LGBTQ bias. Furthermore, because this bias often is fueled by messages from the Christian Right regarding why it is immoral or sinful to be LGBTQ, the stance of neutrality is really a bias toward Christian fundamentalism, arguably making the frame of neutrality-in-schools an extension and masking of the frame of Christianization-in-schools.

Equality

Of course, if the Right really wants to get fundamentalist Christianity and anti-LGBTQ bias into schools, it needs to find ways to include them explicitly in the curriculum, which it is indeed doing. This leads to the third frame, the frame of equality. Advocates of LGBTQ youth are finding ways to introduce lessons on LGBTQ people and issues into the school curriculum, sometimes in lessons on safety and sometimes in the broader context of multicultural education. That is, lessons on LGBTQ people and issues sometimes are included as one of the many dimensions of bias or diversity that make up our schools and society. Not surprisingly, sharp debate ensues over what exactly should be included in a lesson on LGBTQ people and issues, raising the question, Whose perspective should be included?

According to the Right, "multicultural" curriculums often teach students only the perspectives from the Left, resulting in a biased education that silences the perspectives from the Right. A truly multicultural education, it argues, should present a balance of perspectives that reflects "intellectual diversity" and ensures that the Right's perspectives are valued. For this purpose, the Right is mobilizing parents and community members to lobby school boards across the United States to institute several policies that would allow for teaching that there is something wrong with being LGBTQ. One is the "equal time" policy, advanced by the Pro-Family Law Center of the Abiding Truth Ministries (http://www.abidingtruth. com), which includes a provision that

> When issues related to sexual orientation theory, homosexuality, bisexuality, trangenderism [sic], or other alternatives to monogamous heterosexuality within marriage are addressed to students in any manner or form in which these conditions or behaviors are presented as normal, legitimate or harmless, that equal time and access shall be provided to those who oppose this perspective.

When "equal time" is not given to the Right, parents should be able to censor education. Such is the case with the "opt-out" policy, already instituted in various school districts across the United States, which allows parents to pull their children out of lessons on, as the Pro-Family Law Center puts it, "objectionable instruction and materials," particularly regarding sexual health and/or sexual orientation. This is also the case with the more restrictive "opt-in" policy, in which parents must give permission in order for students to attend such lessons.

Censorship of either perspective is not the answer. Students need to learn to think independently and critically, which requires that they learn alternative perspectives to their own and be able to critically analyze the assumptions and implications of any perspective, theirs or others. This requires learning perspectives from the Left, the Right, and points in between. But "equal time" without critical analysis is not the answer either. The notion that opponents should be able to teach what they want if supporters are teaching what they want presumes that the messages from both sides are somehow equal.

The problem, of course, is that this relies on a narrow understanding of equality, one that does not take context into consideration. The "supporting" message and the "opposing" message are qualitatively different. Whereas one message challenges bias against one group of people in society, the other message reinforces and justifies that bias, and therefore has a significantly different impact. As legal scholar Mari Matsuda (1996) has argued regarding freedom of speech, contextual issues of impact and power must be considered when deciding on which type of speech should be protected. Not all speech deserves protection because some speech, such as hate speech, reinforces bias more than others and in so doing, carries a very different potential or power to harm. Inclusion of any perspective must entail a critical examination of its role in reinforcing and challenging bias. This means that, yes, various perspectives should be included in the curriculum, but not in ways that ignore their role in oppression. Unless contextualized, the notion of "equal time" merely provides justification for advancing or simply failing to challenge messages that homosexuality is wrong. In this way, the frame of equality-in-education helps to move forward and mask the ideology of homosexuality-as-deviance.

Truth

Fourth is the frame of truth. Conferences and resources produced by the Christian Right mobilize not only adults, but also youth. For example, Exodus Youth, in addition to organizing conferences, distributes the booklet *Truth and Tolerance: A Youth Leader's Resource for Addressing Homosexuality* (n.d.), which explains the Christian Right's perspective on what is wrong with being LGBTQ, and includes advice for youth on starting "Truth and Tolerance" clubs to counter the gay–straight alliances that already have been formed and continue to be formed in thousands of middle and high schools across the country. Whereas GSAs support LGBTQ youth and challenge anti-LGBTQ bias, the "Truth and Tolerance" clubs reinforce messages that there is something wrong with being LGBTQ and aim to change LGBTQ youth into straight ones. Similarly, the Rightist Alliance Defense Fund recently began sponsoring the annual Day of Truth (http://www.dayoftruth.org), a response to the annual Day of Silence. The Day of Silence was first observed over 10 years ago as a student-led event to raise awareness of the silencing of LGBTQ people in schools and society, and grows each year, reaching over 4,000 campuses in 2006. The Day of Truth claims to offer an alternative view of LGBTQ people, the "truth" of what is wrong with them and how they can be helped.

In both the "Truth and Tolerance" clubs and the Day of Truth, the Christian Right's version of "truth" is supported by controversial, pseudoscientific research claiming that homosexuals can and should be made straight. Such claims have been refuted by major psychological and education organizations, including the American Psychological Association (see *Just the Facts About Sexual Orientation and Youth: A Primer for Principals, Educators, and School Personnel*, available at http://www.apa.org/pi/lgbc/facts.pdf). The Christian Right's "truth" also is supported by quotations from the Bible that seem to condemn homosexuality or gender transgression. Manuals for both the "Truth and Tolerance" clubs and the Day of Truth rely primarily on three quotations:

- "Do not practice homosexuality; it is a detestable sin" (Leviticus 18:22).
- "For this reason God gave them up to degrading passions. Their women exchanged natural intercourse for unnatural, and in the same way also the men, giving up natural

intercourse with women, were consumed with passion for one another. Men committed shameless acts with men and received in their own persons the due penalty for their error" (Romans 1:26–27).

- "Do you not know that the wicked will not inherit the Kingdom of God? Do not be deceived: Neither the sexually immoral nor idolaters nor adulterers nor male prostitutes nor homosexual offenders nor thieves nor the greedy nor drunkards nor slanderers nor swindlers will inherit the Kingdom of God. And that is what some of you were. But you were washed, you were sanctified, you were justified in the name of the Lord Jesus Christ and by the Spirit of our God" (1 Corinthians 6:9–11).

As is characteristic in Christian fundamentalism, these quotations are interpreted by a literal reading, which is a reading in which the words and text mean whatever they mean to someone reading them today in our culture. The text, in other words, is taken as transparent, as literal, as in no need of historical or cultural contextualization. Statements about homosexual acts are upheld as evidence that the Bible, and God, condemn homosexuality. The problem here is not merely that the Christian Right is being selective in its applications to life today, as by decrying the sinfulness of some things listed in the Bible but not many of the other things listed as similarly sinful, like eating certain kinds of food or with certain kinds of people, wearing certain kinds of clothes, or speaking in certain ways about others. In other words, the problem is that the Christian Right is attributing meanings to the Bible without contextualizing the interpretation.

Texts are always contextual, as is apparent when we see that the same phrase can mean different things depending on who spoke it, to whom, when and where, for what purpose, and with what cultural referents, figurative devices, plays on words, innuendos, and so on. For example, when I was growing up my friends and I would call things that we liked "bad," as in "I loved that movie; it was *baaad*," and yet, in the next sentence, we could be talking about a song that we did not like, calling it a bad song and knowing which definition of bad we meant. Similarly, when I lived abroad, my host family would greet my friends and remark on how fat they looked, which was meant as a compliment because of the poverty surrounding the village where we lived; fatness took on cultural meaning as a symbol of prosperity, whether or not the person was prosperous or even very large. Without such contextualization, the phrase can too easily be misunderstood. Thus there is the need for any text to be given a "historical-critical reading" through which the reader tries to understand what it meant to the people who wrote it at that time and in that place (Helminiak, 1994).

Biblical scholar Daniel Helminiak (1994) gives an example of multiple readings of the story of Sodom (Genesis, 19). In this story a man named Lot urges two angels, who appear as men, to spend the night in his house. The male citizens of Sodom demand that Lot give them his visitors so that, presumably, they may use them for sex. Lot refuses. The angels then urge Lot to leave Sodom because God soon will destroy it. A literal reading would conclude that God punished the Sodomites for same-sex sexual activity. However, a historical-critical reading would consider that, in that context, offering hospitality to strangers was one of the most important values in Lot's society and that male-on-male rape was condemned as a form of sexual abuse. So the sin of Sodom was not homosexuality but abuse, offense against strangers, and inhospitality to the needy. Indeed, later references in the Bible to the sin of Sodom refer to inhospitality, not homosexuality.

Not surprisingly, there exist multiple interpretations of the Bible and heated disagreement, even among Christians, over what the Bible means, including what is "true" about homosexuality. Christian fundamentalists, however, have a much easier job of conveying their interpretation as "the" interpretation. After all, it is difficult and counterintuitive for others to argue that the Bible does not condemn homosexuals when faced with a litany of quotations that seem to state otherwise.

This initiative to teach the "truth" to youth is not unlike the efforts by advocates of LGBTQ people to correct the misinformation, stereotypes, and so forth that youth bring to schools. The Right also is concerned about the responsibility of schools to correct what they perceive to be misinformation. But rather than directly saying that their goal is to teach that homosexuality is a sin, the Right has capitalized on more compassionate language: curing, preventing, protecting, saving, helping, educating. So, in turning from the frame of sinfulness-of-homosexuality, the Right has appropriated the language of the Left to frame its work around the truth-about-homosexuality and, in doing so, masks its real message.

In all four of the central frames—innocence, neutrality, equality, and truth—the Right's appropriation and extension of frames from the Left have not changed its underlying messages, as illustrated in Figure 3.1. But such appropriation has allowed the Right to mask its underlying purpose and, consequently, communicate its messages in ways that bring more people on board with its initiatives. Sometimes the Right has been so successful at framing an issue that the Left has had a difficult time reframing and refocusing.

FIGURE 3.1. Appropriation of Frames

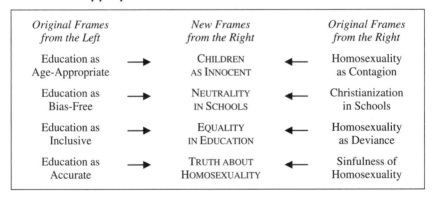

Original Frames from the Left		*New Frames from the Right*		*Original Frames from the Right*
Education as Age-Appropriate	→	CHILDREN AS INNOCENT	←	Homosexuality as Contagion
Education as Bias-Free	→	NEUTRALITY IN SCHOOLS	←	Christianization in Schools
Education as Inclusive	→	EQUALITY IN EDUCATION	←	Homosexuality as Deviance
Education as Accurate	→	TRUTH ABOUT HOMOSEXUALITY	←	Sinfulness of Homosexuality

CHAPTER 4

Failure to Reframe the "Achievement Gap"

Across the U.S., a gap in academic achievement persists between minority and disadvantaged students and their white counterparts. This is one of the most pressing education-policy challenges that states currently face.

—National Governors Association

This all-out focus on the "Achievement Gap" moves us toward short-term solutions that are unlikely to address the long-term underlying problem.

—Gloria Ladson-Billings, 2006, p. 4

GAPS IN ACHIEVEMENT

For decades, researchers have used the term "achievement gap" to describe the difference in levels of educational achievement and attainment for different groups of students in the United States, particularly by race. At times defined narrowly as the gap between White and Black students, the "achievement gap" has come to be understood more broadly as the gap between the higher levels of achievement and attainment among White and Asian American students and the lower levels among Black, Latino/a, Native American, and Alaska Native students (Native Hawaiian and other Pacific Islander students sometimes are grouped with Asian Americans, and at other times grouped with other students of color).

According to the 2005 National Assessment of Educational Progress (National Center for Education Statistics, 2005a, 2005b), a significant gap exists between the achievement of White and Asian/Pacific Islander students and that of other students on standardized tests in reading and mathematics. Among fourth graders, average scale scores in mathematics for Asians/Pacific Islanders were 251 and for Whites, 246, whereas scores for American Indians/Alaska Natives were 226, for Hispanics, also 226, and for Blacks, 220. Among eighth graders, scores for Asians/Pacific Islanders were 295 and for Whites, 289, whereas scores for American Indians/Alaska Natives were 264, for Hispanics, 262, and for Blacks, 255. Average scores were not available for Asians/Pacific Islanders and American Indians/Alaska Natives until recently, but for the past 15 years this gap has been evident between Whites and Blacks/Hispanics with little change. The same can be said of reading scores. Among fourth graders, the average scale scores for both Whites and Asians/Pacific Islanders were 229, whereas the scores for American Indians/Alaska Natives were 204, for Hispanics, 203, and for Blacks, 200. Among eighth graders, the scores for both Whites and Asians/Pacific Islanders were 271, whereas the scores for American Indians/Alaska Natives were 249, for Hispanics, 246, and for Blacks, 243.

A similar gap persists for educational attainment. According to the 2000 U.S. Census (Bauman & Graf, 2003), the percentage of adults aged 25 and older who completed high school or college varies significantly by race. The percentages for graduation from high school were 86% of Whites and 80% of Asians, compared with 73% of Blacks, 71% of American Indians/Alaska Natives, and 52% of Hispanics. In addition, 44% of Asians and 27% of Whites graduated from college and received a bachelor's degree, compared with 14% of Blacks, 12% of American Indians/ Alaska Natives, and 10% of Hispanics. This gap is also apparent when looking at those who take advanced placement examinations; who enroll in honors, advanced placement, and "gifted" classes; and who are admitted to colleges and graduate and professional programs (Ladson-Billings, 2006).

Efforts to explain and address this gap certainly have been on the rise. According to the ERIC and JSTOR databases of published research, hundreds of research journal articles and books have appeared over the past few decades that examine reasons for the persistence of the achievement gap and possible strategies to "close" it. In contrast to any assumption that racial or cultural inferiority is the cause of this gap, explanations often center on the low quality and availability of resources. Black and Latino/a students tend to sit in schools with crumbling walls, outdated or inadequate instructional materials, and underprepared staff. One implication of this research is that, with better resources, these students too can learn and achieve.

In just the past few years, hundreds of presentations have been given at education conferences, from general education research conferences like the annual meeting of the American Educational Research Association (http://www.aera.net), to Leftist conferences like the annual meeting of the National Association for Multicultural Education (http://www.nameorg.org), to conferences that focus specifically on the achievement gap (the Internet search engine Google.com reveals dozens of conferences that featured the theme of the achievement gap). An increasing number of organizations have taken up the achievement gap as a component of their work, including the National Education Association (http://www.achievementgaps.org), which publishes research and resources and conducts trainings for school employees. Some organizations focus specifically or predominantly on the achievement gap, including the research center Achievement Gap Initiative at Harvard University.

More and more educational institutions are treating the achievement gap as a central aspect of their work. School districts and professional associations across the country are offering workshops on the achievement gap. Some institutions of higher education are addressing the gap in their strategic plans, as is the case in one college of education that aims to strengthen its connections to the surrounding urban school system by preparing and supporting teachers who are finding innovative and effective ways to improve education for Black and Latino/a students, the group of students who dominate the school system but whose levels of achievement and attainment are disturbingly low.

As an increasingly diverse group from the Left has undertaken more research and advocacy, the concept of the "achievement gap" has been complicated and expanded. A gap exists not only between White and Black students, but also among other racial groups. A gap also exists within groups along such distinctions as socioeconomic status, gender, language, ability, and ethnicity. This last category is particularly salient for Asian Americans and Pacific Islanders, whose comparatively high levels of achievement and attainment as a racial category mask the vast differences within. One could argue that an achievement gap exists within the Asian/Pacific Islander category that is as wide as or wider than the White–Black gap. According to the 2000 U.S. Census, 44% of Asians graduated from college, compared with 14% of Native Hawaiian and other Pacific Islanders. Furthermore, while 44% of the larger Asian population graduated from college, only 8% of refugee Southeast Asian Americans (namely, Cambodians, Hmong, and Laotians) graduated, which is a rate even less than those for Black, Hispanic, and American Indian/Alaska Native adults.

Even economically, there is a vast gap within the Asian/Pacific Islander category. According to the 2000 U.S. Census, this group had a higher median household income than any other group, including Whites. But this statistic is misleading. Asian/Pacific Islander households were larger in size than the national average, resulting in a per capita income thousands of dollars less than that for Whites. Furthermore, the higher median household income must be balanced with the higher rates of poverty for certain ethnic groups. Native Hawaiians and other Pacific Islanders were living in poverty at almost one-and-a-half times the national average, and Cambodians, Hmong, and Laotians, at almost two-and-a-half times. Native Hawaiians, Pacific Islanders, and refugee Southeast Asian Americans seem more like the other racial groups than the high-achieving Asian/Pacific Islander group that is supposed to include them.

Some scholars and advocates have argued that this diversity among Asian Americans and Pacific Islanders requires a disaggregation of data and a more accurate representation of their educational experiences. Such was the argument in a report on the education of Asian Americans and Pacific Islanders issued by the National Education Association that resulted from a national summit on this topic that I co-organized (Lee & Kumashiro, 2005), as well as other publications that include Asian Americans in discussions of the achievement gap (see, for example, Paik & Walberg, 2007). Not all Asian Americans and Pacific Islanders are succeeding educationally and economically, and therefore they too have a stake in closing the achievement gap.

THE DEMAND TO ASSIMILATE

But the solution should not be merely to close this gap. There are many ways of conceptualizing the "problem" of race and education, and as with any conceptualization, the "achievement gap" has its strengths and weaknesses. In particular, it focuses on only a part of the problem. Gloria Ladson-Billings (2006) makes this argument when comparing education to the national budget. In any given year, the federal government struggles to balance its budget and to avoid a budget deficit where the amount spent exceeds its income. Over time, these deficits add up to a national debt that has increased steadily over the past 2 centuries to its current level of $8 trillion. Financed by government borrowing, this debt requires almost $133 billion in interest each year, which helps to explain why, even in those years that the United States has had a balanced budget, the national debt continued to grow. Heated public debates between political parties over "pork" spending that prevents a balanced budget mask the larger problem of the steadily increasing national debt and interest payments. Annual budget deficits, in other words, are merely a part of a much larger problem.

So, too, with the achievement gap. Ladson-Billings (2006) argues that "our focus on the achievement gap is akin to a focus on the budget deficit, but what is actually happening to African American and Latina/o students is really more like the national debt. We do not have an achievement gap; we have an education debt" (p. 5). From its history of differentiating education by race, to its current system of unequal funding by district, the education system has worked to disadvantage certain groups, accumulating an "education debt" that makes the achievement gap inevitable. Raising test scores does not solve the larger problem of this education debt. And perhaps that's the point. Perhaps the focus on the achievement gap is a distraction that allows the larger inequities to persist.

In fact, attempts to "close the gap" actually can fuel the problem. The language itself suggests that the goal is simply to bring up those below the gap; that is, to make the lower achieving groups more like the higher achieving ones. This implies that White and Asian American students are learning what students are "supposed" to learn and that they define success in school. But this is not necessarily the case among Asian Americans, the group that is considered by some to be "outwhiting the Whites" in levels of achievement. To say that the goal is to close the gap between the lower achieving Pacific Islanders and refugee Southeast Asian Americans, on the one hand, and other Asian Americans on the other, suggests that the high-achieving Asian Americans are doing fine and should be considered the model for the other Asian Americans and Pacific Islanders who are failing. Research on Asian Americans in U.S. schools tells a very different story, one in which even high-achieving Asian Americans are facing problems (Lee & Kumashiro, 2005). The achievement gap is not the only way that racism manifests. From subtle cultural mismatches and biases in the curriculum to blatant discrimination and violent acts of harassment, Asian American students reveal a range of ways that racism plays out, even for students who are achieving. This includes internalized forms of racism (Osajima, 1993), as when Asian American students believe that they are supposed to be the model student, which some researchers suggest is a primary reason why Asian American young girls have the highest rates of severe depression and, according to the U.S. Department of Health and Human Services (Cohen, 2007), why Asian American young women have the highest rates of suicide of any race.

Clearly, students learn a range of things in schools, making the "academic" things inseparable from cultural context and political conflict. For this reason, almost a century ago, Carter G. Woodson in *The Mis-Education of the Negro* (1933/2006) argued against educating Black students as we educated White students. Delineating a range of ways in which the education system privileged Whiteness and Eurocentric knowledge and perspectives, he argued that Black students were being "mis-educated" so as to assume subservience in a racist society. The problem was not about how much different students were learning and that Black students were learning less than White students; the problem was *what* all students were learning and that *all* students were learning in ways that perpetuated oppressive ideologies. Feminists have made similar critiques of the male-centeredness of curriculum; queer theorists, of the heterosexism in curriculum; and critical theorists, of the fostering of a particular class-consciousness (Pinar, Reynolds, Slattery, & Taubman, 2000). Raising the achievement of historically marginalized students in the current education system is counterproductive if what is being taught is biased to begin with.

So, too, with how schools assess what is being taught and learned. Test scores are not the only things that should matter in education, if for no other reason than that test scores do not tell all. Standardized tests measure only certain types of learning, particularly rote learning, and as educators push to raise test scores and "teach to the test," other types of learning, including critical and creative thinking skills, get marginalized. Furthermore, standardized tests can be culturally biased, as when answers presume that students share the White middle-class cultural referents of the test makers (like, "cup goes with saucer"), or when questions are dropped from the test because not enough of the White middle-class test group can answer them correctly. After all, standardized tests are piloted and revised based on how the target audience of primarily White and middle-class students responds, thus ensuring that the norm-referenced system of scoring maintains the higher achievement levels of those who historically have done well. Students with different cultural referents, learning styles, and language skills are disadvantaged from the beginning, and only as they assimilate to the presumed norm do they raise their chances of achieving (Sleeter, 2005).

Yet test scores increasingly are dominating popular discourse on education reform, as when newspapers publish average test scores for schools, as well as policy initiatives by both the Right and the Left. Nationwide, attention to test scores and the achievement gap increased with the passage of NCLB. NCLB requires that test scores be disaggregated by race in order to show which groups are being underserved by schools in a particular area, and then ties rewards and sanctions to schools and school districts based on their "annual yearly progress," particularly in raising low scores and closing gaps. Even critics of NCLB like the National Education Association have argued that one of the positive aspects of NCLB is its attention to and publicizing of research on racial disparities in achievement.

On the surface, the attention to the achievement gap seems like a positive step toward improving education, but it is also a strategic move by the Right in its attack on public education, for several reasons. First, the achievement gap gives those on the Left a reason to join with the Right, and gives the impression that the Right is indeed concerned about students of color and racial inequity. The achievement gap, in other words, puts a compassionate face on the Right's initiatives. Second, the requirement of producing test scores opens myriad opportunities for corporations to profit from school districts and states as they now must purchase testing materials, scoring services, curriculums, and supplemental student services for test preparation. The move toward testing and accountability has fueled the privatization of public education at a time when more and more research is raising questions about the value and validity of such standardized and high-stakes assessments of student learning.

Third, the focus on high-stakes testing has narrowed the curriculum precipitously, as teachers and schools face increasing pressure to raise scores in reading and math, and do so by reducing time for learning other subjects or even developing other knowledge and skills. Teachers are being forced to "teach to the test," and some are further constrained by scripted curriculums for such purposes.

Fourth, the framing of the problem in terms of an achievement gap masks other ways that oppression plays out in schools, from the day-to-day experiences of students with harassment, discrimination, and bias to the larger factors that constitute the "education debt," particularly the structural racism that is exemplified in the historical, economic, and curricular causes of inferior education for students of color. Although the achievement gap is a manifestation of structural racism, it nonetheless distracts from it.

Fifth, and perhaps most important, the focus on an achievement gap puts the blame for school failure on the victim. After all, it is difficult to argue that an achievement gap is the result of structural racism when at least one population of students of color actually is achieving. Time and again, this is reinforced with data, in particular the test scores that often are accepted as the primary indicator of student learning. In other words, the concept of the achievement gap, with Asians/Pacific Islanders on both sides of the gap, enables a collective ignoring of structural racism. The implication is that if some Asian Americans are making it, the problem for all other students of color cannot be structural racism. Rather, the problem must be that either their teachers are not teaching well or the students themselves are not capable of learning.

PURPOSES BEHIND THE "MODEL MINORITY"

This should sound familiar. What makes the achievement gap insidious is its reliance on the "model minority" stereotype of Asian Americans. Popularized by the media in the mid-1960s, the portrayal of Asian Americans as economically and educationally successful (Osajima, 1988) was in stark contrast to images of Black pathology that were described in the highly publicized 1965 report by Daniel Patrick Moynihan, *The Negro Family: The Case for*

National Action, also known as the Moynihan Report (Prashad, 2000). Images of Black pathology also were (mistakenly) attributed to the 1966 report from the U.S. Department of Health, Education and Welfare, *Equality of Educational Opportunity*, also known as the Coleman Report, which focused further national attention on racial disparities (Ladson-Billings, 2006).

Smart, hard-working, obedient, and perseverant, Asian Americans were "whiz kids" in school and achieving the "American dream" as adults. They were models for all minorities, so successful as to be "outwhiting the Whites" (S. J. Lee, 1996, p. 5). The data to back such claims were contested but the image persisted, in large part because of its political significance. At a time of racial unrest and in the middle of the Civil Rights Movement, the model minority stereotype refuted claims of structural racism by upholding a racial minority group that, through hard work, was making it. The thinking was, "if they can make it, so can you."

In the time since, the model minority stereotype has served as a divide-and-conquer strategy to prevent communities of color from coalescing by convincing them that Asian Americans "aren't like other people of color." The stereotype also has prevented the larger Asian/Pacific Islander community from uniting by contrasting the Asian and Pacific Islander ethnic groups above the gap with those below. In fact, the ambiguous and shifting positions of Asian Americans and Pacific Islanders in the U.S. racial hierarchy reflect the importance of protecting the boundaries around and between a Black–White conceptualization of race relations. The 1992 riots in Los Angeles following the Rodney King verdict are illustrative. Korean American merchants in primarily working-class Black communities were considered by some Whites to be like Blacks in that they were merely "minorities" or second-class citizens, and were considered by some Blacks to be like Whites in their economic privilege and outsider status. This split perspective served to reify a Black–White racial conflict rather than illuminate a much more complex set of relations that were inseparable from social class, immigration status, and other social markers (Cho, 1993). Korean American merchants were impacted by the political economy and racial divides in the communities in ways both similar to and different than their Black neighbors, and yet they were positioned as model minorities and therefore not as possible allies in the struggle against racism or poverty.

When put alongside the Black–White racial hierarchy, the model minority stereotype "de-minoritizes" (S. S. Lee, 2006) Asian Americans, as can be seen in the achievement gap that pairs minority status with low achievement, and similarly in debates about affirmative action in higher education that pair minority status with underrepresentation in enrollment. In both cases, Asian Americans do not count as minorities.

When framed as model minorities, Asian Americans sometimes have remained silent, or spoken only as allies to other groups of students, claiming that "we stand by you." In either situation, Asian Americans seem unsure of whether they have the right to speak or even an audience interested in hearing them speak about problems experienced by Asian American students that pale in comparison within the frame of the achievement gap. At other times, Asian Americans have spoken out to explain that not all Asian Americans are achieving and that "we, too, are oppressed." The call to disaggregate data by ethnicity to illustrate the lower academic achievement of Native Hawaiians, other Pacific Islanders, and refugee Southeast Asian Americans is one such example. But even in this situation, the model minority stereotype masks the deeper problem of structural racism. Like the frame of the achievement gap, the stereotype of the model minority frames the "problem" in terms of a single group's experiences, as when asking why Blacks, or Pacific Islanders, or other groups are not achieving as well as Asians. The "success" of some Asians allows deeper problems to remain unexamined, particularly the various contributors to the "education debt." As Matsuda (1996) has argued, Asian Americans need to be saying, "We will not be used."

Historically, the image of Asian Americans as the model minority has been used variously in service to White privilege, corporate interests, and U.S. imperialism. In the 1940s, some Chinese Americans distinguished themselves from Japanese Americans and presented themselves as the "good Asians" so as not to bear the brunt of anti-Asian racism that increased during World War II and manifested in the internment of Japanese Americans (Wong, 2005). Some Japanese American young men chose to enter the U.S. military to show that they were indeed model U.S. citizens and not spies or traitors loyal to the enemy (Okihiro, 1994). In the 1940s and 1950s, the U.S. State Department sent Asian American celebrities to Asia as ambassadors of good will, primarily to present a positive image of life for Asians in capitalist America in the midst of several interrelated phenomena: the Cold War, the threat of increasing communization of Asia, and the emerging U.S. dominance over the global market (Lui, 2007).

Domestically in the 1950s, the image of Asian Americans as a racially marked immigrant group that was successfully integrating into U.S. society played an important role in countering tensions arising from mainstream society's unwillingness to integrate three other forms of difference, namely, the "three specters that haunted Cold War America: the red menace of communism, the black menace of racial integration, and the white menace of homosexuality" (R. G. Lee, 1999, p. 10). Beginning in the 1960s, the popular press portrayed Asian Americans as economically and educationally successful, as evidence that people of color were not exempt from the American dream, and such portrayals continue to dominate the media and the research literature today (Ng, Lee, & Pak, 2007). Beginning in the 1980s, particularly in California, debates around affirmative action in higher education involved images of the Asian American, model minority student, particularly by opponents of affirmative action who claimed that Asian Americans would be victims of affirmative action admissions policies because, already overrepresented in some institutions, their enrollment numbers would end up being capped (Takagi, 1992). Like other stereotypes, the model minority is a construction that can be and has been deployed for a range of political purposes, racial or otherwise.

At different points in U.S. history other stereotypes of Asian Americans emerged, all serving to reinforce hierarchies of race, social class, gender, and nationality. Within popular culture, at least six representations of Asian Americans can be seen: the "pollutant" was an alien presence in the idealized image of a racially pure Westward expansion; the "coolie" was a laborer subservient to and in competition with White labor preceding and during industrialization; the "deviant" was a figure of forbidden sexual desire and a threat to racial purity in the household; the "yellow peril" was an invader that threatened national security, wealth, and worldwide dominance, first during periods of restricting immigration, and later during wars with Asian nations; the "model minority" was a model for all other minorities; and the "gook" was an invisible enemy, particularly as envisioned during the Vietnam War (R. G. Lee, 1999). Another stereotype that is commonly experienced by Asian Americans in everyday interactions is that of the "perpetual foreigner," or the Asian American who is always more Asian than American. This stereotype is evidenced by such comments as, "You speak English really well," or the question, "Where are you from?" (and if you say, "Chicago," the follow-up question, "No, where are you really from?"), which fail to distinguish Asians from Asian Americans, many of whom were born and raised in the United States (S. J. Lee, 1996).

These various stereotypes often overlap and reinforce one another. This happens in schools (Ng, Lee, & Pak, 2007) as it does in broader society, as historian Gary Okihiro (1994) explains.

> The concepts of the yellow peril and the model minority, although at apparent disjunction, form a seamless continuum. While the yellow peril threatens white supremacy, it also bolsters and gives coherence to a problematic construction: the idea of a unitary "white" identity. Similarly, the model minority fortifies white dominance, or the status quo, but it also poses a challenge to the relationship of majority over minority. The very indices of Asian American "success" can imperil the good order of race relations when the margins lay claim to the privileges of the mainstream. (p. 141)

Stereotypes get deployed variously and strategically, often in consort with another, in ways that reinforce White privilege and mask structural racism. As a result, we fail to see not only the complexity of the situation, but also our own complicity and responsibility to act.

FRAMING AWAY OUR COLLECTIVE RESPONSIBILITIES

The power of stereotypes to mask deeper problems was certainly apparent in a recent tragedy involving an Asian American student that captivated the nation in the spring of 2007, namely the shootings at Virginia Tech University. The tragedy reminded me of 5 years earlier when a student at the college where I was teaching was killed on the outskirts of campus by another young adult who was not a college student. In mourning and in search of an explanation, people felt somewhat comforted by framing the killer as evil or as an outsider. But many of us also felt uncomfortable at the simplicity of such explanations, which perhaps only fueled tensions between an elite campus and an impoverished surrounding community, and prevented us from healing.

Too often our explanations of tragedies distract from the underlying problem. In the 1990s the fatal shootings at Columbine High School and other schools incited heated debates about violence in video games and rock music, the availability of weapons and how-to manuals, and the presumed shortcomings of parents and communities. The nation seemed perplexed by this sudden rise in violence, even though, according to the U.S. Center for Disease Control, the rate of violence on school grounds actually was going down. Glaringly absent was discussion of the decreasing rates of school violence at a time of increased media attention, perhaps because the shootings were taking place in different types of communities with different types of victims, affecting "middle" America rather than poorer communities of color. Also absent was discussion of what most of the boys who committed the shootings experienced daily in their schools, namely bullying and harassment in the form of being called "fag" or "queer" (Kimmel & Mahler, 2003). Bullying has become an epidemic in our nation's schools, commonly taking the form of anti-gay harassment that targets not only students who are gay, but also students who are in any way different. Yet too often such harassment goes unchallenged by educators. By framing the shootings as singular acts of "boys gone bad," we failed to understand the role of bullying and thus evaded our collective responsibility for changing it.

As investigations continued into the troubled life of the student, Seung-Hui Cho, who committed the shootings at Virginia Tech, we learned that Cho, too, was bullied in school, taunted and isolated because of his race, his nation of origin, his language background, and his social class. We commonly see victims of bullying and other forms of abuse respond in a variety of ways, at times withdrawing, but at times acting out as perpetrators of abuse toward others. This being so, when we heard that Cho was accused of stalking and sexually harassing women on campus, we should have been outraged at the persistence of violence against women and social apathy around it, and we should have echoed the research on violence against women by insisting that we address broader social dynamics, including cycles of abuse and a culture of violent masculinity, rather than conclude simply that Cho was "evil" or "mean."

How we frame a story matters, and within hours of the Virginia Tech shootings the framing was quite clear: The shooter was a Korean immigrant. In the news stories to follow, certain images of Cho persisted, including that he was an immigrant, "resident alien," from a devout Christian family, a smart student, quiet student, unknown student, but a student who was capable of harassment and who harbored ideas of extreme violence. These images mapped onto three of the most common stereotypes of Asian Americans, namely the "model minority" who is quiet and hardworking, the "perpetual foreigner" who will never fully fit in, and the "yellow peril" who is a threat to the well-being of Americans. This mapping made it quite easy to hear stories about Cho and then interpret them to be stories that reflect Asian Americans in general, or at least what the stereotypes would have us fear that Asian Americans are capable of.

A powerful way in which the media influences the general public is by tapping into stereotypes and prejudices. This has been the case throughout history as different communities faced backlash in the wake of tragedies that seemed to implicate them, such as Japanese Americans in the wake of Pearl Harbor or Muslim Americans in the wake of 9/11. Not surprisingly, soon after the media began identifying the shooter as this Korean immigrant, Asian American leaders began voicing fears of reprisals against Asian Americans, and such fears were quickly realized. I received reports from schoolteachers and counselors about incidents of taunting and harassment of Asian American students who were being told to go back to Korea, whether or not they were recently immigrated or even of Korean ancestry. Ironically, in response to the tragedy at Virginia Tech, Asian American youth experienced the kinds of anti-Asian harassment that Cho experienced in his youth.

Some Asian Americans apologized for the actions of one of their own. Other Asian Americans distanced themselves from Cho, arguing that he was not representative of Asian Americans, that he was mentally ill, or that he was evil. But not many Asian Americans were saying that this tragedy pointed to larger problems within schools and society, particularly of oppression based on race, class, gender, sexuality, and other markers that plague our nation's schools. The framing of this tragedy helped to mask these larger problems, and instead fueled stereotypical ways of thinking about racial difference, perpetrators of violence, and responsibility for change.

Frames have the power to shape society's understanding of and responses to problems, whether they are tragic events like campus shootings or persisting injustices like the education debt. Too often such conversations are framed in ways that prevent a deep understanding and the collective will to act. To truly address inequities in education, the American people must engage different frames.

CHAPTER 5

Frames for a Broader Left

> Our frames shape our social policies and the institutions we form
> to carry out policies. To change our frames is to change all of this.
> Reframing *is* social change.
>
> —George Lakoff, 2004, p. xv, emphasis in original

A few years ago I had a student teacher who struggled immensely with classroom management. She found it difficult to keep her mixed-ability classes focused and engaged, and at times the students were quite disrespectful. The student teacher expressed to me her hope that, when teaching full-time, she would be assigned an honors-level class of students who were mature and engaged enough to make classroom management a non-issue. Such a class, she believed, would be one in which she could really teach. In response, I asked her whether teaching was something that happened only when students behaved in certain ways, namely in ways we often think that "good" students are supposed to behave? Was it a problem, in other words, to think that good classroom management preceded real teaching? Some of the theories we read in class suggested that student engagement can have everything to do with what and how we teach, and that, in fact, wanting and expecting students to be students in only certain ways might lie at the heart of teaching "problems."

That same year I taught a seminar where several student teachers complained that anti-oppressive education (education that challenged multiple forms of oppression) seemed impossible. There were so many complexities of oppression, so many contradictions of activism, so many nuances in what and how we teach, and given that even the "expert" (the professor) was still exploring what it could mean to teach in anti-oppressive ways, and given that every approach to anti-oppressive education seemed to have weaknesses, they wondered whether they would ever know enough to teach anti-oppressively. In response I asked them whether anti-oppressive teaching is something that happens only when all of the complexities are known, when all the contradictions are prevented, and when all the weaknesses are addressed. Was it a problem, in other words, to require that teachers come to a full understanding of oppression and teaching before they feel comfortable teaching anti-oppressively? Was it a problem to define anti-oppressive teaching as only those instances of teaching that were not, in some ways, problematic? Some of the theories that we read in class suggested that anti-oppressive education is not something that happens when the contradictions and partialities are gone, but instead is exactly what happens when we are working through these "problems." In fact, some of the theories that we read in class suggested that approaches to teaching that presume to be unproblematic are the very approaches that we want to critique. I wondered aloud: Perhaps it is the expectation that anti-oppressive teaching happens only in ideal situations that makes teaching feel so impossible and suffocating. For my students, the barrier to imagining and engaging in anti-oppressive education was not the failure to understand its complexities, but rather the desire to overlook them. They resisted the practice of anti-oppressive teaching as long as they framed anti-oppressive education as only that which happens without contradiction.

In a similar way, the challenges experienced by the Left can be understood in large part as a result of its inability to address the contradictions of anti-oppressive activism. That is, historically, civil rights movements have experienced challenges in coalition building and institutional and cultural change when they failed to address the contradictions inherent in such work, within education and beyond. New frames that can build a broader coalition on the Left, therefore, must address contradiction.

THE RIGHT TO BE DIFFERENT

Contradictions are certainly apparent in civil rights law, raising questions about exactly what type of "progress" has been made historically. Legal scholar Kenji Yoshino (2002) argues that society often measures its progress against various forms of oppression by the degree to which it prohibits—legally and culturally—overt forms of discrimination. In particular, society often considers itself to have made progress when it moves from demanding that differences be "converted" or changed, to demanding that differences be "passed" or hidden (that is, passed as something else), to allowing differences to coexist as long as they are "covered" or downplayed. This progression from the demands to convert, to pass, to cover characterizes dominant views of the history of gay rights in the United States, for example. The thinking goes something like this: Whereas LGBTQ people once were expected to be converted or cured, they are now being asked to pass or hide, as with the military's "don't ask, don't tell" policy, and in some contexts are even allowed to be out as LGBTQ if they do not make their LGBTQ-ness obvious, such as by refraining from cross-dressing, public displays of affection, or mention of their same-sex partners or desires.

One problem with this model of progress is that it sets up hierarchies among the different forms of assimilation—with conversion being the most severe—as well as the different groups in society targeted by these assimilationist demands. In particular, those groups that experience discrimination because of traits considered to be immutable or necessarily visible—including people of color and women—have been deemed more in need of legal protection from discrimination than groups that presumably can change or at least hide. Of course, the distinction between groups that are visibly marked and those that are not is not always very clear. Racial and gender differences are not always apparent, as with people of color who "look White," and sexual orientation is not always hidden, as when LGBTQ people "act gay" through dress, mannerism, and affiliation. Furthermore, researchers continue to debate what can and cannot be changed about oneself, including sex and sexual orientation. But even if we accept that some differences are unchangeable and apparent, it is not the case that all forms of discrimination target the differences that we cannot change or hide. In fact, discrimination today often targets what we *can* change. Like LGBTQ people, people of color and women are expected to cover or downplay their differences all the time, as when they are expected to lose an accent, wear only certain clothes, style their hair in only certain ways, and behave in gender-appropriate ways. Antidiscrimination laws protecting citizens from demands to convert or pass often fail to protect against demands to cover.

While these more subtle forms of discrimination may seem less severe than demands to convert or pass, the demand to cover can impact the very core of a person's identity as severely as the other demands. That is, the demand to cover can be a demand to downplay those things that lie central to one's sense of self. This becomes clear with the recognition that identities and differences are not embedded in bodies, but rather are developed in relation to other identities and differences. Who a person is has much to do with how that person relates to others, which means that a person's sense of self has much to do with how others read that person, from the immutable bodily traits (like skin color) to the mutable acts and ways of being (like speaking with or without an accent). By failing to protect what people can change about themselves, particularly those things that mark them as different, antidiscrimination laws indirectly require that differences be assimilated, since only with assimilation will people avoid discrimination.

Civil rights law, like the broader civil rights movements, can be seen to have made progress, but only partially so. Behind the surface of protection lies the insidious demand to assimilate, which renders quite problematic any objective claims of progress. What needs protection is not merely our *inability* to change (as when we find ourselves a cultural minority), which by implication means that those things that can be changed, should be changed. Rather, what needs protection is our *ability* to change (as when we express our cultural pride) so that we are free to be different than what the mainstream society says we ought to be. What needs to change are not the differences among us, as if assimilation were the cure to all social ills, but rather the ways that we read those differences, the demands we make of those differences, and our complicity with their assimilation. Yoshino (2002) argues, "Civil rights practice, after all, is fundamentally about who has to change: The homosexual or the homophobe? The woman or the sexist? The racial minority or the racist?" (p. 938). The shift from protecting what we cannot change to protecting what we can, is simultaneously a shift from changing those people who are different from the norms to changing the norms themselves and the ways that they regulate who we can be.

Therein lies the potential to draw together a much broader coalition. Many people have experienced the demand to downplay their differences from racial, gender, and other norms, and many therefore may be willing to coalesce against the privileging of these norms. After all, no one entirely and always conforms to these norms, and even if someone did, such an exception would be irrelevant because the point here is that no one should have to entirely and always conform.

Across the multiple dimensions of diversity (race, gender, etc.) and within the various aspects of schooling (curriculum and instruction, student services and extracurricular activities, school culture and school–community relations, school organization and staffing), it is not difficult to find examples of how schools demand the assimilation of difference. By reframing education reform around the right to be different, the Left can redefine "civil rights" as something that protects all of us, not only those in the minority.

OPPRESSION HURTS EVERYONE

For the Left to succeed, it is vital to broaden the conversation to show how oppression hurts everyone. As legal scholar Derrick Bell (2005) argues, advances in civil rights must take into account the concept of "interest convergence," which is the notion that Whites have supported racial advances for Blacks only when such advances have served the interests of Whites. This was the case in the 1954 U.S. Supreme Court ruling in *Brown v. Board of Education*, often heralded as a major advance toward racial equality because of its ban on segregation in schools, but made possible in large part because of the Cold War and the need for the United States to eliminate legal segregation in order to improve its image internationally. In fact, Bell argues that the compromised ruling in *Brown* did more harm than good for Black students, as evidenced by the enduring failure of the U.S. education system to serve Black students. Perhaps this should not be surprising: To reach interest convergence, compromises and sacrifices must be made, particularly by those who have more to gain by the compromise (for example, Blacks), which means that in the end, policies will always meet the priorities of the policymakers or, more accurately, will always best serve the interests of those in power (in this case, Whites).

Civil rights law historically has been framed as a benefit to the disadvantaged, as with its protection from discrimination against those differences that cannot be changed. But Yoshino's proposal to protect people any time that they differ from norms means that those who benefit from civil rights law would be anyone who does not conform, including those who historically have been privileged. Whites can experience discrimination if they reflect stereotypes of "white trash" or the "dumb blond"; men can experience discrimination if they do not dress or speak or walk or act in a "properly" masculine way; heterosexuals can experience discrimination if they do not date the "right" type of person or opt for the "right" type of living arrangement. After all, there are "proper" or "desirable" ways to be White, to be a "real" man, to be straight, and while these social expectations and values can vary by context, they nonetheless bring sanctions even to the historically privileged groups when they do not conform. Whites, men, and heterosexuals also would benefit from protections against the demand to downplay their differences.

Until now, the Left's work on LGBTQ issues in education has been framed primarily as an issue about LGBTQ people and, indeed, as I travel around the country and deliver workshops on LGBTQ issues

I am often told of straight allies who wanted to attend the workshops but did not do so for fear that they would be seen as gay, as if only gay people care about such issues. One way to reframe LGBTQ issues and make them "everyone's issue" is to shift from focusing on homophobia and the marginalizing of LGBTQ students to focusing more broadly on oppression and how it hurts everyone.

LGBTQ students are not the only ones who are harmed by homophobia. Also harmed are children with LGBTQ family members or friends, children who are questioning their own identities, children who are themselves doing the bullying, and children who may not identify as LGBTQ but who nonetheless endure homophobia because they do not look, act, or in some way present themselves as gender norms dictate that they "should." This last category is the largest and perhaps the most significant because it reminds us that all students experience pressures to present themselves in certain ways in order to avoid being teased or ostracized. As illustrated by the pervasive use of "faggot," "queer," and "dyke" toward boys who are not "masculine enough" or girls not "feminine enough," homophobia polices the boundaries around what is acceptable regarding sexual orientation and gender identification for all students, not only LGBTQ ones (Kimmel, 1994). Indeed, in the highly publicized school shootings in the 1990s, the boys who committed the shootings endured daily harassment and slurs of "faggot" and "queer" even though none of them self-identified as gay (Kimmel & Mahler, 2003). To avoid homophobia we exert enormous energy trying to conform to what we think we are supposed to be, and through homophobia we punish everyone, including ourselves, when we do not or cannot.

Homophobia, therefore, is not the only problem. What also needs illumination and critical examination are the norms themselves that are guarded by homophobia, namely the images and rules of who and what and how we are supposed to be that we are trying so hard to police. Challenging these norms is often difficult because they are hard to see, hidden behind the language of what is natural, normal, appropriate, or moral. One of these norms is heterosexism, the system of ideas and practices that privilege heterosexuality via the notion that people are supposed to be heterosexual and that with the appearance of heterosexuality comes many benefits, not only legal and economic but social and moral as well. Challenging heterosexism is not about saying that heterosexuality is wrong; rather, it is about saying that heterosexuality is not the only way to be. This is important even for people who are heterosexual, because heterosexism often comes entangled with other regulations, including those regarding romance, marriage, procreation, and, of course, relations between men and women.

This leads to the related topic of gender norms and the notion that people are supposed to be a certain way depending on their bodily sex. Being a "man" often means that a person should look, walk, talk, feel, interact, and produce certain things in certain ways or risk being called a "girl," a "sissy," or a "fag." So, too, with being a "woman." There are social expectations, rules to follow, and sanctions for those who do not or cannot conform, and these can change over time and differ depending on the racial, ethnic, socioeconomic, religious, and other social/political contexts in which we find ourselves. Important here is the notion that the sanctions primarily take the form of homophobia, which helps us to understand why homophobia may target students who do not conform to gender norms (regardless of their sexual orientation) more than it targets students who self-identify as gay or lesbian (Horn, 2007).

The shift of focus from the oppression of some to the oppression of all simultaneously shifts the kinds of questions that education reform would ask, from "How do we protect LGBTQ students from encounters that oppress sexual difference?" to "How do we protect all students from encounters that privilege particular notions of sexual normalcy?" Or from "How do we get students of color to learn as White students learn?" to "How do the very things that all students are currently learning and the ways that their learning is assessed advantage some groups and disadvantage others, and how do we change such things?" In so doing, the Left can reframe education reform in ways that show how challenging oppression would benefit all, including those groups that historically have been privileged.

MULTIPLE HUMAN RIGHTS

Perhaps one of the biggest challenges to forming a broad coalition of the Left is the contradiction inherent in anti-oppressive activism itself. Saying what and who you are fighting for requires simultaneously saying what and who you are not fighting for, which means that any approach to challenging oppression cannot help but to create new margins. This can happen simply when defining who is privileged and who is marginalized. The binaries of male/female and of hetero/homo, for example, force individuals to choose sides, masking the possibility that bodies can be male, female, or intersexed; sexual orientations can be heterosexual, homosexual, or bisexual. The third, in-between possibilities often are erased forcibly, as when a medical professional surgically and hormonally alters intersexed bodies that are sexually ambiguous but otherwise healthy into ones that are more clearly or properly male or female. Even those who are marginalized in the gender/sexual binaries sometimes contribute to the erasure of third possibilities, as when activism around forced medical procedures on intersexed bodies has confronted resistance from some feminists, who question how intersexuality and the disruption of the category of "women" will impact the feminist movement (Chase, 1998). Similarly, the stereotype that bisexuals are confused or merely on their way to becoming fully homosexual pervades lesbian/gay communities, not only straight ones. This notion that bisexuality does not exist reflects the unspoken agreement between straights and gays that bisexuality must not exist, lest the privilege of heterosexuality as well as the advances made by "gay politics" be challenged (Yoshino, 2000).

My point here is that even the identity and activism of those on the margins can be framed and thus limited by gender and sexual norms, helping to explain why activism can fracture the very communities it aims to serve. The experiences of groups that lie at the intersection of multiple communities are illustrative. For decades, Black feminists have pointed to ways in which antisexism movements that claim to work for all women can unintentionally and indirectly reinforce White privilege, as when White women dominate the decision-making processes and overlook ways in which women of color can experience sexism differently. On the flipside, they have pointed to ways in which antiracism movements that claim to work for Blacks can unintentionally and indirectly reinforce male privilege, as when Black activists say that any public criticism of sexism among Black men works against Black solidarity and should be curbed (hooks, 1994). Similarly, LGBTQ people of color experience oppressions at the intersections of difference, as with heterosexism within communities of color and racism within LGBTQ communities. Such a reinforcing of oppressions even within activist communities points to the problem of assuming that each group can address only "its" issue and that such separation is possible and desirable, as when expecting LGBTQ activists to address heterosexism and people of color to address racism, without doing anti-oppressive work within each community. In fact, the failure of these two communities to do their own internal work helps to explain why the gay marriage issue was able to serve as such a powerful wedge in the 2004 presidential elections, particularly as Republicans tapped into conservative churches to draw out communities of color to vote for candidates who shared their opposition to gay marriage.

The problem, of course, is that oppression is rarely about "only" one form of difference. Racial ideologies have always been gendered and sexualized, and vice versa. It is not possible to understand "traditional Asian values" without noting how they revolve around the heterosexual family, traditional gender roles, and procreation, as when saying that the virtuous Asian is one who gets married, has children, and passes down the family name (Kumashiro, 2002). It is not possible to understand the category of "ladies" without noting how, historically, being a "lady" was limited to females who were White and middle class (Higginbotham, 1992). Even today, idealized masculinity as reflected in the media overwhelmingly consists of men who appear to be White, heterosexual, and able-bodied (Kimmel & Mahler, 2003). Oppression is not merely "the sum of its parts," which means that activism cannot be approached additively. Anti-oppressive activism must address intersections.

The Left increasingly has faced difficulties addressing intersections. Duggan (2003) argues that the emergence of neoliberalism as the operative ideology in U.S. politics in the 1980s and 1990s coincided with the fracturing of the Left into two main camps: cultural or identity politics and the fight for rights of particular groups on the one hand, and class or progressive politics and the fight for changes in the U.S. political economy on the other. Both are needed and both have advanced the civil rights movements, but neither can bring about systemic change alone and neither can build the broad-based coalitions needed for sustained work. Both need to rally around the bigger picture.

The Civil Rights Movement originally had a broader goal. In the 1940s and 1950s the leading civil rights organizations strategized ways to take before the new United Nations Commission on Human Rights charges that the United States was violating the human rights of its Black citizens, as evidenced by the pervasiveness of poverty, the inferiority of their educational and healthcare provisions, and their disenfranchisement from government (Anderson, 2003). However, in response to historical and political forces, including the Cold War and fears of being called communist as well as the power of the Southern Democrats and their influence over the White House, they changed strategy, retreating from the broader human rights agenda to the civil rights measures we see today that focus on the right to be free from discrimination and treated equally in public sectors. The civil rights organizations were able to make legislative and cultural changes, but largely because of a compromised agenda.

The original goal of broader, multiple human rights has the potential to go much beyond the right to be treated equally. It encompasses various other rights, framed by the expectation that every human being has worth and value and dignity, not only in the ways that we are similar but also, and perhaps more important, in the ways that we are different. Loretta Ross (2006), founder and former executive director of the National Center for Human Rights Education, describes eight categories of human rights.

- *Civil rights*: the right to be treated as an equal
- *Political rights*: the right to fully engage in a participatory democracy
- *Economic rights*: the right to live and work in an economy that meets the needs of all people
- *Social rights*: the right to receive quality health, human, and education services from the government
- *Cultural rights*: the right to practice the culture of one's choosing
- *Environmental rights*: the right to live in healthful environments
- *Development rights*: the right of people in developing countries to control their own natural resources
- *Sexual rights*: the right to determine one's sexuality and control one's body

Advocating for one type of rights should not take away from the other rights. Rather, when strategized as a component of a larger movement, advocacy for any of the rights should reinforce and align with the other components. Quality education is a right for all people, but because schools do not exist in a vacuum, advocating for education rights must intersect with advocacy for political, economic, social, developmental, and environmental rights. Similarly, schools are a context in which other rights can be denied, and therefore advocating for education rights must intersect with advocacy for cultural, civil, and sexual rights. By envisioning education reform in the context of a broader human rights movement, the Left can bring together a coalition that is often fractured and uncoordinated.

The Right has been successful at addressing multiple issues and framing its initiatives in ways that mask its intentions, divide and conquer the Left, and bring many from the middle on board. The Left must respond in kind. It must address multiple issues, frame its initiatives in ways that amplify its broader goals of human rights, understand and learn from the Right about the power of framing, and, in the process, lead the American people toward anti-oppressive reform. Education in the United States can look very different if framed by *the right to be different*, the recognition that *oppression hurts everyone*, and the bigger picture of *multiple human rights*. These are frames that challenge the undermining of public education already underway and that embody the values of the American people. The time for us to reframe public education has come. I look forward to seeing the changes that result.

References

American Civil Liberties Union. (2001). *Surveillance under the USA PATRIOT Act*. Retrieved September 9, 2007, from http://www.aclu. org/SafeandFree/SafeandFree.cfm?ID=12263&c=206

Anderson, C. (2003). *Eyes off the prize: The United Nations and the African American struggle for human rights, 1944–1955*. New York: Cambridge University Press.

Apple, M. W. (2001). *Educating the "right" way: Markets, standards, God, and inequality*. New York: Routledge.

Aziz, N. (2004). The Right's attack on faculty, programs, and departments at U.S. universities. *The Public Eye, 18*(1). Retrieved September 9, 2007, from http://www.publiceye.org/magazine/v18n1/aziz_campus.html

Bauman, K. J., & Graf, N. L. (2003). *Educational attainment: 2000, Census 2000 brief*. Washington, DC: U.S. Census Bureau.

Bell, D. (2005). *Silent covenant:* Brown v. Board of Education *and the unfulfilled hopes for racial reform*. Oxford: Oxford University Press.

Blount, J. (1996). Manly men and womanly women: Deviance, gender role polarization and the shift in women's school employment, 1900–1976. *Harvard Educational Review, 66*(2), 318–338.

Britzman, D. P. (1998). *Lost subjects, contested objects: Toward a psychoanalytic inquiry of learning*. Albany: State University of New York Press.

Butler, J. (1993). *Bodies that matter: On the discursive limits of "sex."* New York: Routledge.

Carlson, P. (2001, September 23). California's Barbara Lee under attack for opposing war powers resolution. *Pittsburgh Post-Gazette*, p. 4.

Carr, N. (2006). *Spread the word: Campaign is a sham. "65-percent solution" to school funding seeks to advance a partisan political agenda*. Retrieved September 9, 2007, from http://www.eschoolnews.com/news/show Story.cfm?ArticleID=6197

Chase, C. (1998). Hermaphrodites with attitude: Mapping the emergence of intersex political activism. *GLQ: A Journal of Gay and Lesbian Studies, 4*(2), 189–211.

Cho, S. K. (1993). Korean Americans vs. African Americans: Conflict and construction. In R. Gooding-Williams (Ed.), *Reading Rodney King/ reading urban uprising* (pp. 196–211). New York: Routledge.

Chon, M., & Yamamoto, E. K. (2003). *Resurrecting Korematsu: Post-September 11th national security curtailment of civil liberties.* Retrieved September 9, 2007, from http://www1.law.ucla.edu/~kang/race rightsreparation/Update__Ch__8/update__ch__8.html

Cianciotto, J., & Cahill, S. (2003). *Education policy: Issues affecting lesbian, gay, bisexual, and transgender youth.* New York: National Gay and Lesbian Task Force Policy Institute.

Cianciotto, J., & Cahill, S. (2006). *Youth in the crosshairs: The third wave of ex-gay activism.* New York: National Gay and Lesbian Task Force Policy Institute.

Coen, J. (2001, October 9). Hate-crime reports reach record level. *Chicago Tribune*, p. 11.

Cohen, E. (2007). *Push to achieve tied to suicide in Asian-American women.* Retrieved September 9, 2007, from http://www.cnn.com/2007/ health/05/16/asian_suicides/index.html

Cohen, H. S. (Producer), & Chasnoff, D. (Producer & Director). (1996). *It's elementary: Talking about gay issues in school* [Film]. (Available from Women's Educational Media, 2180 Bryant Street, Suite 203, San Francisco, CA 94110)

de Moraes, L. (2005, January 27). PBS's 'Buster' gets an education. *The Washington Post*, p. C1.

deMarrais, K. (2006). "The haves and the have mores": Fueling a conservative ideological war on public education (or tracking the money). *Educational Studies, 39*(3), 201–240.

Duggan, L. (2003). *The twilight of equality? Neoliberalism, cultural politics, and the attack on democracy.* Boston: Beacon Press.

Eng, D. L. (2001). *Racial castration: Managing masculinity in Asian America.* Durham, NC: Duke University Press.

Epstein, D., O'Flynn, S., & Telford, D. (2001). "Othering" education: Sexualities, silences, and schooling. *Review of Research in Education, 25*, 127–179.

Exodus Youth. (n.d.) *Truth and tolerance: A youth leader's resource for addressing homosexuality.* Retrieved September 9, 2007, from http://exodus youth.net/youth/curriculum.html

Fay, G. R. (2004). *AR 15-6 Investigation of the Abu Ghraib Detention Facility and 205th Military Intelligence Brigade.* Retrieved September 9, 2007, from http://www.yuricareport.com/PrisonerTortureDirectory/General Fay82504rpt.pdf

Fuller, B. (2003). Education policy under cultural pluralism. *Educational Researcher, 32*(9), 15–24.

dson-Billings, G. (2006). From the achievement gap to the education debt: Understanding achievement in U.S. schools. *Educational Researcher, 35*(7), 3–12.

koff, G. (2004). *Don't think of an elephant: Know your values and frame the debate.* New York: Chelsea Green.

e, R. G. (1999). *Orientals: Asian Americans in popular culture.* Philadelphia: Temple University Press.

e, S. J. (1996). *Unraveling the "model minority" stereotype: Listening to Asian American youth.* New York: Teachers College Press.

e, S. J., & Kumashiro, K. K. (2005). *A report on the status of Asian Americans and Pacific Islanders in education: Beyond the "model minority" stereotype.* Washington, DC: National Education Association.

e, S. S. (2006). Over-represented and de-minoritized: The racialization of Asian Americans in higher education. *InterActions: UCLA Journal of Education and Information Studies, 2*(2), Article 4. Retrieved September 9, 2007, from http://repositories.cdlib.org/gseis/interactions/vol2/iss2/art4

man, P. (2004). *High stakes education: Inequality, globalization, and urban school reform.* New York: Routledge.

g, C. A. (2000). Reading, writing, and reconstruction: The Christian Right and the politics of public education. *Educational Policy, 14*(5), 522–637.

g, C. A. (2001). The Christian Right: A cultivated collection of interest groups. *Educational Policy, 15*(1), 41–57.

M. (2007, February). *Selling the model minority abroad: Narratives of racial progress in America's cold war cultural diplomacy.* Paper presented as a public lecture at the University of Illinois–Chicago.

cedo, M., & Steinberg, S. R. (Eds.). (2007). *Media literacy: A reader.* New York: Peter Lang.

suda, M. J. (1996). *Where is your body? And other essays on race, gender, and the law.* Boston: Beacon Press.

re, M. (Producer & Director). (2004). *Fahrenheit 911* [Film]. (Available from Columbia Tristar Home Entertainment, 10202 W. Washington Boulevard, Culver City, CA 90232)

onal Center for Education Statistics. (2005a). *National Assessment of Educational Progress, The Nation's Report Card: Mathematics 2005.* Washington, DC: U.S. Department of Education.

onal Center for Education Statistics. (2005b). *National Assessment of Educational Progress, The Nation's Report Card: Reading 2005.* Washington, DC: U.S. Department of Education.

onal Governors Association. (2005). *Closing the achievement gap.* Retrieved September 9, 2007, from http://www.subnet.nga.org/nuclear/achievement/

Helminiak, D. A. (1994). *What the Bible really says abc
Recent findings by top scholars offer a radical new vie*
Alamo Square Press.

Higginbotham, E. B. (1992). African-American women'
metalanguage of race. *Signs: Journal of Women in Cu
17*(2), 251–274.

hooks, b. (1994). *Teaching to transgress: Education as the p
New York: Routledge.

Horn, S. (2007). Leaving LGBT students behind: Schoo
rights. In C. Wainryb, J. Smetana, & E. Turiel (Eds
ment, social inequalities and social justice (pp. 131–15
Erlbaum.

Horowitz, D., & Lehrer, E. (n.d.). *Political bias in the admin
ulties of thirty-two elite colleges and universities.* Retriev
2007, from http://frontpagemag.com/content/read.
Isaac, A. P. (2006). *American tropics: Articulating Filipino
apolis: University of Minnesota Press.

Johnson, C. (2000). *Blowback: The costs and consequences of
New York: Henry Holt.

Kaneko, L. (1976). The shoyu kid. *Amerasia Journal, 3*(2),
Kimmel, M. S. (1994). Masculinity as homophobia: F
silence in the construction of gender identity. In
Kaufman (Eds.), *Theorizing masculinities* (pp. 119-
Oaks, CA: Sage.

Kimmel, M. S., & Mahler, M. (2003). Adolescent masculin
and violence: Random school shootings, 1982–2001.
ioral Scientist, 46(10), 1439–1458.

Kirkpatrick, D. D. (2005, January 20). Conservatives pick
toon sponge. *The New York Times*, p. A16.

Klein, D., & Stern, C. (2004). How politically diverse are tl
and humanities? Survey evidence from six fields. *Ac
18*(1), 40–52.

Kosciw, J. G., & Diaz, E. M. (2006). *The 2005 National Scho
The experiences of lesbian, gay, bisexual and transgender yo
schools.* New York: Gay, Lesbian, and Straight Educati

Krehely, J., House, M., & Kernan, E. (2004). *Axis of ideol
foundations and public policy.* Washington, DC: Nationa
Responsive Philanthropy.

Kumashiro, K. K. (2002). *Troubling education: Queer activis
sive pedagogy.* New York: Routledge.

Kumashiro, K. K. (2004). *Against common sense: Teaching ar
social justice.* New York: Routledge.

NCATE. (2006). *A statement from NCATE on professional dispositions.* Retrieved September 9, 2007, from http://www.ncate.org/public/0616_MessageAWise.asp?ch=150

Ng, J. C., Lee, S. S., & Pak, Y. K. (2007). Contesting the model minority and perpetual foreigner stereotypes: A critical review of literature on Asian Americans in education. *Review of Research in Education, 31,* 95–130.

Okihiro, G. (1994). *Margins and mainstreams: Asians in American history and culture.* Seattle: University of Washington Press.

Osajima, K. (1988). Asian Americans as the model minority: An analysis of the popular press image in the 1960s and 1980s. In G. Y. Okihiro, S. Hune, A. A. Hansen, & J. M. Liu (Eds.), *Reflections on shattered windows: Promises and prospects for Asian American studies* (pp. 165–174). Pullman: Washington State University Press.

Osajima, K. (1993). The hidden injuries of race. In L. A. Revilla, G. M. Nomura, S. Wong, & S. Hune (Eds.), *Bearing dreams, shaping visions: Asian Pacific American perspectives* (pp. 81–91). Pullman: Washington State University Press.

Paik, S. J., & Walberg, H. J. (Eds.). (2007). *Narrowing the achievement gap: Strategies for educating Latino, Black, and Asian students.* Cambridge, MA: Springer.

Phillips, S. (2006, February 16). *"The 65 percent solution": School finance proposal energizes and alarms.* Retrieved September 9, 2007, from http://www.connectforkids.org/node/3914.

Pinar, W. F. (Ed.). (1998). *Queer theory in education.* Mahwah, NJ: Erlbaum.

Pinar, W. F. (2001). *The gender of racial politics and violence in America: Lynching, prison rape, and the crisis of masculinity.* New York: Peter Lang.

Pinar, W. F., Reynolds, W. M., Slattery, P., & Taubman, P. M. (2000). *Understanding curriculum: An introduction to the study of historical and contemporary curriculum discourses.* New York: Peter Lang.

Prashad, V. (2000). *The karma of brown folk.* Minneapolis: University of Minnesota Press.

Prashad, V. (2006). The global war against teachers. *Radical History Review, 95,* 9–20.

Rofes, E. (2005). *A radical rethinking of sexuality and schooling: Status quo or status queer?* Lanham, MD: Rowman & Littlefield.

Ross, L. (2006). *Plenary speech.* Retrieved September 9, 2007, from http://www.thetaskforce.org/downloads/events/CC/LorettaRoss_PlenarySpeech_CreatingChange2006.pdf

Rudalevige, A. (2003). The politics of No Child Left Behind. *Education Next, 3*(4), 63–69.

Said, E. (1979). *Orientalism.* New York: Vintage Books.

Sanday, P. R. (1990). *Fraternity gang rape: Sex, brotherhood, and privilege on campus.* New York: New York University Press.

Save Senn Coalition. (n.d.). *A letter to citizens of the 48th ward and CPS families re: the Navy takeover of Senn High School.* Retrieved September 9, 2007, from http://www.savesenn.org

Sleeter, C. E. (2005). *Un-standardizing curriculum: Multicultural teaching in the standards-based classroom.* New York: Teachers College Press.

Smith, S. (2001). *The democratic potential of charter schools.* New York: Peter Lang.

Standard & Poor's. (2005, Fall). *The issues and implications of the "65 percent solution." SchoolMatters: A service of Standard & Poor's.* Retrieved September 9, 2007, from http://www.schoolmatters.com

Takagi, D. (1992). *The retreat from race: Asian American admissions and racial politics.* New Brunswick, NJ: Rutgers University Press.

Taylor, H. (2001). *Overwhelming public support for increasing surveillance powers and, in spite of many concerns about potential abuses, confidence that these powers would be used properly.* Retrieved September 9, 2007, from http://www.harrisinteractive.com/harris_poll/index.asp?PID=260

Tyack, D., & Tobin, W. (1994). The 'grammar' of schooling: Why has it been so hard to change? *American Educational Research Journal, 31*(3), 453–479.

U.S. Department of Education. (2002). *PL 107-110 The No Child Left Behind Act of 2001.* Retrieved September 9, 2007, from http://www.ed.gov/policy/elsec/leg/esea02/index.html

Wheeler, T. (2003, July 12). Parents fight Jeb's biased test. *People's Weekly World Newspaper.* Retrieved September 9, 2007, from http://www.pww.org/article/view/3725/1/171/

Wong, K. S. (2005). *Americans first: Chinese Americans and the Second World War.* Cambridge, MA: Harvard University Press.

Woodson, C. G. (2006). *The mis-education of the Negro.* San Diego, CA: Book Tree. (Original work published 1933)

Yoshino, K. (2000). The epistemic contract of bisexual erasure. *Stanford Law Review, 52*(2), 353–461.

Yoshino, K. (2002). Covering. *Yale Law Journal, 111,* 769–939.

Younge, G. (2006, April 4). Silence in class. *Guardian.* Retrieved September 9, 2007, from http://www.guardian.co.uk/usa/story/0,,1746227,00.html

Index

About the Author

Kevin K. Kumashiro, Ph.D., is an associate professor of policy studies at the University of Illinois–Chicago, College of Education, and the founding director of the Center for Anti-Oppressive Education (http://antioppressiveeducation.org) where he develops resources for members of educational communities interested in creating and engaging in anti-oppressive forms of education. He has worked as a teacher and teacher educator in public and private schools and colleges in the United States and abroad, and has served as a consultant for various schools, school districts, and state and federal agencies. He has authored or edited several books, including *Six Lenses for Anti-Oppressive Education: Partial Stories, Improbable Conversations* (2007, co-edited with Bic Ngo), *Against Common Sense: Teaching and Learning Toward Social Justice* (2004), *Troubling Intersections of Race and Sexuality* (2001), and *Troubling Education: Queer Activism and Antioppressive Pedagogy* (2002), which received the 2003 Gustavus Myers Outstanding Book Award.